JUGGLING WITH FINESSE

BY KIT SUMMERS

Edited by Robert Schwarz
Artwork by Tuko Fujisaki

Learn to juggle! It's great fun and good exercise.

Kit Summers

JUGGLING WITH FINESSE

©Copyright 1987 Kit Summers

Published by
FINESSE PRESS
2068 Via Las Cumbres, Suite 7
P. O. Box 11244
San Diego, California 92111

Library of Congress Cataloging in Publication Date

ISBN number 0-938981-00-5

Library of Congress Catalog Card Number: 86-091875

Printed in United States of America

TABLE OF CONTENTS

FOREWORD BY DICK FRANCO

With the ever increasing number of jugglers developing the world over, it is only natural to expect the appearance of a book not only aimed at the beginning juggler, but also at the already accomplished juggler as well. Up until now, most juggling instruction books were written for the beginner, and meant to carry them through only the basic forms of juggling. Occasionally the last chapter might be devoted to a few so called BIG TRICKS for the really ambitious or adventuresome juggler, but in general the appeal has been to the novice.

The result of this has been thousands of basically well-trained but technically mediocre jugglers, frustrated by the lack of stimuli to progress further. Without the aid of some kind of outside influence (books, magazines, films, or other jugglers) it is difficult for any juggler to progress past a certain point. A book of this type is therefore very valuable.

Numbers juggling, i.e. juggling with 5 or more objects, has up until the last few years been considered by many to be a sort of no man's land to the amateur or hobbyist juggler. This type of juggling was left to the seasoned working professional. I have often seen a person struggling with 4 balls and would suggest that they try 5 or even 6 for a half an hour or so, the reason being that 4 balls are a lot less confusing after handling 5 or 6 for a while. As they take the extras in hand you can see the grip of fear set in. My theory has always been...to do more makes it easier to do less, so by all means practice numbers, if only to improve the juggling you are presently doing.

I believe that correct mental attitude is the most important requisite if you seriously want to learn advanced juggling, the object being to downplay the difficulty of each attempted trick. Certainly it is much more difficult to juggle 7 balls than 3, but if you make up your mind to learn 7, and convince yourself that it is not going to be all that difficult, half the battle is won and the steps toward learning will be much less painful.

I can think of four important words which apply to learning numbers. DESIRE...PERSISTENCE...CONCENTRATION...AND PATIENCE. DESIRE is the most important. If you don't have the REAL DESIRE to spend the thousands of hours it takes to learn each trick you will never be a numbers juggler. Second in importance is CONCENTRATION. The amount of concentration you put on each try will determine how long it will take you to learn that particular move. If you have HONEST DESIRE, persistence and patience will automatically develop...and a few years of PRACTICE...and the result will be the lifelong SATISFACTION you get being an advanced juggler.

This book is dedicated to Bobby May, whose kindness and skill at juggling were an inspiration.

ACKNOWLEDGEMENTS

I want to thank some of the people that in one way or another helped me in writing this book. When I first began writing, I didn't know what a gigantic project I was taking on. I showed JUGGLING WITH FINESSE to many people for criticism and comments, much of which I included in the book. Some of the people that I would like to give heartfelt thanks to are the following:

Dick Franco, for inspiring me to be a juggler when I first began, and for writing the foreword for the book.

Martha Smith, my college English teacher, who guided me in the beginnings of the book and also helped me with some finishing touches.

Mary Ellen King, who did the final corrections on the book, and for bringing so much joy into my life.

Elizabeth Summers, Mom, who put up with a lot from me after I had the accident, and the rest of my family, Kath, Gary, and Mike.

Robin Summers, for support and some spelling and wording advice.

Thea Klein, who taught me to use the word processor.

Robert Nelson, who helped me in many ways, and also gave me inspiration to work hard on the book and keep going with it.

There were others who have helped me in one way or another, either in support or ideas. Many people have contributed to my juggling education and to the book. I am grateful to them all: Mark Neisser, Jon Held, Charlotte and Lorna Paris, Ben Decker, Daniel Holzman, Paul Kyprie, Bill Giduz, Jack Wiley, Ken Benge, Nick Gatto, Ron Graham, Joe Buhler, Chris Bayly, Carrie Topliffe, Barry Friedman, Peter Davidson, Kathy Recchia, Joe Maiorano, and Kings Printing.

Printed by KNI
Typesetting by the Type Factory, La Mesa, California

PREFACE

JUGGLING! Life is like juggling. Now and then you drop, then you pick up and continue. That's the story of my life. It was a challenge which I met initially in 1975 at the age of sixteen because I am inevitably intrigued by unusual things. The difficulties any beginner must face in getting started only goaded me on to redouble my efforts with the happy consequence that my skills rapidly improved. After only two years, I had become proficient enough to make it to the The Gong Show, where I received $500 for placing first, doing something I really enjoyed. No more timely reward could have presented itself. There I was on the very edge of show business, admittedly bedazzled more than a bit. It was at that point that I decided to become a professional. Undaunted by the otherwise sobering reality of the many hours, weeks, months, possibly years that it would require to attain the technical mastery and confidence demanded for professional stage performance. I literally immersed myself in the world of juggling, going to Hawaii in 1978 to practice and perform with my good friend Barrett Felker, who later became a featured juggler with the Harlem Globetrotters. It was while in Hawaii that I began my collection of juggling memorabillia and pictures, examples of which appear in this book. That trip was a great learning experience for me which culminated toward the end of the year when I toured Europe to research jugglers and juggling, and also to see what type of acts were selling. By the following year, I was teaching juggling for the 1979 session of Ringling Brothers and Barnum and Bailey Clown College. From a sixteen year-old beginner back in San Diego, I had circled half the globe, discovered and perfected my talents, and in four short years found myself bemusedly a kind of professor! It was all dizzying and in retrospect a trifle hilarious.

In 1981, I began performing in and around San Diego an act which I called "Juggling with Finesse." This visibility led to my first big break which came in September of 1981. I was booked at Bally's Park Place Casino in Atlantic City, New Jersey. Although I was initially scheduled to perform in the cabaret for one month, the management liked my work so well that they extended my contract for nine months. I had passed from the edge into the very limelight of show business. My juggling at this point was at a high level and I was trying to master juggling 7 clubs, a world record at that time. However, I attempted this feat not for publicity but rather for personal satisfaction. I never actually thought of performing the 7 clubs in my act. I mention this to underscore that in juggling you can probe your own potentialities and grow in a special way as the reach of your talent stretches outward. This stretching and knowing that you are constantly expanding in what you can do gives you a security all your own, a security that none can challenge because you, and you alone sometimes, know how far you have reached in perfecting this unique aspect of yourself.

If I can call this stretching and growing the deeper facet of juggling, it is this facet, this resource which helped me to surmount the great tragedy which befell me on the night of April 3, 1982. I was walking to work probably engrossed in thought, contemplating some detail of my act, closed in upon myself against a dreary rain, shrouding street lights and stop signs in a shiny blur. Suddenly, out of the downpour, from behind a sheet of rain, a truck sped upon me, struck me, hurling me into a coma which held me fast in unconsciousness for 37 days. Altogether, I stayed in the hospital for four months. Through some miracle, my mind remained intact, but the strings between it and my body were cut. The normal commands to move could not make my marionette body respond. I had to learn once again to eat, talk, walk, and juggle — basically everything. I still had the knowldedge of what to do, but I had to retrain my body to move to my inner commands. It was as if my mind was put into a mannequin, and I had to train that inanimate object to perform all the tasks necessary for normal life. Knowing what to do and how to do it, yet not being able to do it produced extreme frustration. But I had faith that in time I could relearn my lost skills; I just wanted time to move faster.

As I struggled to regain my former skills, I made progress by setting specific goals for myself. While working within a schedule of due dates, as it were, when each task had to be completed. Thus, step by step, I was able to fulfill my schedule of goals and on Sunday, April 3, 1983, exactly one year after my accident, I performed once again in San Diego's Balboa Park. When working previously in Balboa Park, I noticed that the best day of week on which to perform was Sunday. It was as if it were meant to be that I should perform that very day, one year after the accident. That was a big goal to be reached in my retraining schedule. I began by telling my friend Randy Foster, who used to perform with me, my idea. He was enthusiastic about it. Bolstered by his support, I sat down and worked out a stage show based on the skill level that I had regained at that point. Generous pre-show publicity from the local media brought many people to witness my comeback to juggling. The show went well although I could not be happy that my juggling ability failed to match my expertise before the accident. I couldn't stop comparing my present skill level to my previous, world record level of juggling. To conclude the show we passed torches around a volunteer from the crowd. Despite the disappointment at my reduced expertise, I felt really good about having done the show. I could tell that people were sincerely happy to see me out there again. That night I had a party at my house. It was a, "We're-glad-we're-all-alive" party, a fitting name for the celebration. I had a wonderful time that day. In a sense, I was born again. Ironically, not to something new, nor to some exotic faith, but to a part of what I once was. For me that was a rebirth as miraculous as any I could realistically conceive.

I have described my comeback from the accident in terms of the highlights of progress, perhaps giving the idea that it happened like magic overnight. That's not the case. I know that it's not what happens that determines the quality of a person's life, the difference is what you do about it. The thrill I felt at my first comeback peform-ance was attained only after weeks of work, many hours a day, and with the support of many friends. Through it all, I not only regained some of my former ability to juggle; my belief in the importance of setting goals was reaffirmed. And I shall dwell on this latter point not simply because of its personal significance to me, but also because I feel that it is the key to learning the art of juggling. For me, you see, it was the key to relearning that art. Without setting goals for themselves, people stumble through life, not knowing where they are going, so in the end, they never get any-where. You can't be aimless about it. A Marine General once told my lawyer and friend Tom Vesper that, "whereas the ordinary man gets involved in an action, the hero acts such as to change the course of action. You change the course of action by setting goals and systematically going about achieving them."

Maybe you think this is too lofty a view toward learning to juggle, but take it from one who knows — it is not. I should know, after all, I am one of the few people in the world who learned to juggle...TWICE! Learning to juggle again was a painful process for me, after having been robbed of my skills. It was boring and frustrating to rehearse outwardly what I already knew inwardly to do. I had once mastered the art of juggling with considerable finesse. The neurological pathways from my brain to my limbs had to be rerouted to obey the messages from my mind. As I have said, in my mind all the procedures of juggling were clear; I knew how to move, but my body had to learn once again to comply with that knowledge. When I returned to juggling, I had trouble juggling 3 balls. I dropped them, I fumbled, my body was undisciplined, and I got angry; but I set goals for myself and thereby step by step overcame the obstacles and ultimately changed the course of action from failure to success.

Five months after my injury, my friend Dave Held, helped me to ride a bicycle. I got on, he steadied me, I wobbled, but miraculously the balance was there! The joy I felt must have rivaled that of any five year old as he learned to ride for the first time. A goal was met. Next I tackled the unicycle. I rode in the hallway of my house, steadying myself by holding onto the walls. In a day I was able to ride the unicycle once again. Another goal achieved. I guess it's true when they say: "Once you learn to ride a unicycle you don't forget."

At this time of retraining, I was going to Sharp Hospital in San Diego for my rehabilitation. I was not yet allowed to drive so I rode my bicycle the twenty miles round-trip. This built up my strength as well as honing my coordination. What to others might have seemed a hardship was for me another goal. Next came driving. I have always felt very comfortable behind the wheel of a car and I was determined that that was not going to change. The next International Jugglers Association Convention was scheduled in New York. Attending the convention was to provide another goal — to drive from my home in San Diego to the Convention in New York. Need I tell you! I did it. Once again, I experienced the joy of setting and attaining a goal.

If setting goals helped me to return to juggling, I feel that contrarily juggling played an important role in my recovery. From juggling, I learned self-discipline, concentration and patience, all of which sustained me in my long struggle to reaffirm myself as a whole person. By writing the definitions of how to do the various tricks in this book I could feel myself doing them once again, which was great for me. This is not only a manual to learn juggling for I have tried to include many ideas that can help you with your entire life. Through juggling I was able to improve my strength and dexterity, and this did wonders for my self-confidence. Combined with the natural drive I have always had juggling provided the specific motivation I needed for recovery. Eight months after my injury on a trip back to the East Coast, I visited Dr. Lawrence Strenger, the neurosurgeon who performed my brain surgery. A quotation from his report illustrates the progress of my juggling. "...Kit is able to juggle and ride a unicycle, which is quite remarkable for a person having suffered the injuries he sustained..."

As I look back on it all, and analyze what juggling has meant to me before and after my accident, both mentally and physically, I find myself compelled to share my experience, my utter joy, with others by writing this book. In writing this book I share with you not merely a personal world but a public one as well. For juggling cannot only open you to yourself, it can also open you to the world. At least to the wonderful world of people who juggle and who appreciate juggling. Throughout this book I recount incidents involving jugglers whom I have met. I frequently call them good friends of mine, and so they are. There is no other endeavor with which I am acquainted which has as participants the wonderful people found in juggling. They are generous with their time and assistance for beginners learning the art, and they rally around in time of crisis like family!

I hope first, that through this book I can provide you with the keys to teaching yourself to juggle and thereby open to you ways to master other goals you may set for yourself. Secondly, it is my hope that through juggling you will discover the deepest recesses of your inner potentials by setting goals and refusing to accept less from yourself than your fullest capability. And I know that if you do this and reach out to share yourself with others who are doing the same, you will find yourself a friend among friends in a far richer world than that which you now inhabit.

ONE
INTRODUCTION

Anyone can learn to juggle. Surprisingly, it is not as difficult as it looks to the novice. If you can throw and catch one ball you can learn to juggle. It is just a matter of learning the principles underlying the art, and then putting those principles into practice. As in most other skills, practice is the key. Juggling appears to be a difficult physical skill, and most people think it is beyond their capability. But with some practice, almost anyone can learn to juggle. Juggling is the art of suspending more objects than you have hands. With a good juggling act you can travel into every corner of the globe, play for the people of every country, have the world at your fingertips. Juggling is recognized the world over and is loved by almost everyone. As a sport, juggling builds confidence, concentration, persistence and self-esteem. And finally, juggling is FUN!

Whether a beginning juggler, or a seasoned professional, this book will have something for you. I shall describe for you in detail a whole repertory of juggling moves. They are intended to give a basic description of the tricks so you can work on them by yourself. Juggling is a self-taught art. What I am attempting in writing this book is to open your mind to all of the tricks that can be tried and accomplished with juggling, and maybe even inspire you to think of your own tricks, or things to juggle. I inspire you to think of your own tricks, or things to juggle. I have not put the tricks in an order of difficulty because what might seem hard for one person, might not be for another. If told in advance that something is difficult, many people are discouraged from trying it. Several of the tricks included are ones that I have enjoyed learning and doing myself. There are so many different things to juggle, and ways to juggle, it is virtually unlimited, so there is really no way that I could cover it all. That would take many volumes, and maybe I will be writing a few more books on the subject. There is little written elsewhere on juggling performance; the last chapter deals with performance skills. From this chapter you can learn how to put together a show and turn your juggling into a performance on stage or otherwise before an audience. Above all, have fun with the handling of objects in a dextrous manner.

Some of the tricks that you read about in this book may be hard to comprehend by simply reading, but once you try them you will start to get an understanding of how they are accomplished. Jugglers usually learn the details of different tricks from other jugglers, so you may want to watch for a juggler who can do some of the moves described or attempt to work out details with a juggling partner. Many basic juggling patterns require simple movements and a minimal amount of work. Because of their simplicity, the book will not deal with them. Instead, it explains some moves that you may not think of.

But you must begin with a working knowledge of the principles involved in juggling. It is my desire to contribute to the continuation, expansion, and endless advancement of juggling by providing the novice with a practical step-by-step guide which will take you from beginning moves to the most advanced. Another very good book written on juggling is **THE ART OF JUGGLING,** by my old friend, Ken Benge. This book covers many things from first learning to juggle to many intermediate and advanced moves. You see, juggling is only partially a matter of coordination. It is also a matter of practice, and a thought process, figuring out the best way to do a certain trick. It is a thinking game in which you gain ingenuity by continually figuring out better and better ways to perform your chosen tricks.

I am happy to say that television has helped to popularize juggling in the past decade or so. People see jugglers perform on variety and circus shows, and they begin to feel that maybe they could do some of these things too. And they are right! Because of increased exposure, various tricks that just a few years ago were considered advanced are now being performed not just by a few, but by many jugglers. The annual convention of The International Jugglers Association is held in a different city in the United States annually and has been attracting more people each year. I feel that once people know of different tricks on the advanced level that can be done, then they will tell themselves that they might be able to do them also, with practice. As a result, jugglers are going on to conceive and master feats previously undreamed of or thought impossible. Over the past ten years, juggling has advanced to ever higher levels of difficulty and artistry. We may be experiencing a veritable juggling renaissance!

This sudden advancement is all the more amazing in light of the considerable antiquity of juggling. Jugglers and juggling have entertained people the world over for centuries, from the ancient Egyptians and Romans to the American Indians. Much of this juggling is associated with religious rituals. In the tomb of Beni Hasson, dating from around 1900 B.C., there is a painting of a group of women juggling balls, although some people think it is different views of one woman. The word, juggler, comes from the Latin, **joculator,** a funny fellow, based on the root, **joculari,** a jest. The Latin word, joclator, and its later medieval French equivalent, **jongleur,** both applied to itinerant entertainers who might do anything from singing ballads to performing various feats of legerdemain. These traveling entertainers did not always have the most savory habits, causing Shakespeare to rail against such patchery, such juggling and such knavery!

Drawings of jugglers from around 1900 B.C.

Juggling is known worldwide. I thought it interesting to note some of the spellings for the words juggle and juggler, in different languages from around the world. Here's a sample for word juggle: German — **jongler;** Dutch — **goochelen;** Portuguese — **malabarismo;** Norwegian — **gjore tryllekunster;** Afrikaans — **goel;** Spanish — **escamoteo;** Italian — **giocolar;** Polish — **Kuglarstwo;** Indonesian — **Menyulap;** Latvian — **Trics;** Swahili — **Fanya Kiinimacho.**

For the word juggler: German — **Jogleor;** Portuguese — **Malabarista;** Norwegian — **Tryllekunstner;** Afrikaans — **Goelaar;** Spanish — **Malabarista;** Italian — **Giocoliere;** French — **Jonguer;** Latin — **Praestigiator;** Irish — **Cleasi;** Welsh — **Siwglwr;** Japanese — **Tejina-shi;** Hawaiian — **Kanaka Kilokilo;** Indonesian — **Pemain sunglap;** Rumanian — **Scamator;** Lativian — **Burvju makslinieks;** Swahilil — **Mfanya kiinimacho.**

Webster's English Dictionary defines the word juggle as follows: "1. - To keep several objects in motion in the air at the same time. 2. - to manipulate esp. in order to achieve a desired and often fraudulent end." The second definition is very interesting.

Fortunately, juggling has today become a very respectable art or pastime. It is enjoyable in itself. You needn't be a performer to get the most out of it. You can do it just for fun. It is good for working out as well as for relaxing. Just by bending down to pick up a dropped prop you get good exercise. A half hour of juggling versus a half hour of exercising - the results are the same; the difference: juggling will exercise your mind as well, and improve your mental and physical alertness, coordination, reflexes, eyesight, and self-confidence. It will give you an alert body and a calm mind. Joggers often experience a "high" during their run; juggling is similar in that you can only get better, and acquiring new tricks is quite stimulating. Always let your reach exceed your grasp and persist until you succeed at whatever it is that you want to accomplish. As a sport, juggling is open ended. You will never reach a limit of what you can do. With juggling you can act as your own audience. It's a self-testing behavior in which your reward may be your own achievements. In sports such as golf or bowling, you can top out more easily than with juggling. With juggling you can never say, "Now I know everthing about it." There is always one more prop that can be added to the pattern or one more trick to learn. Always try to expand your goals as soon as the old ones are attained. With many sports you may be able to cover up an error, but dropped props speak for themselves. Juggling is a good training of eye-hand coordination for players in every sport. It improves accuracy in throwing, and confidence in catching. I know of one basketball team that learned to juggle to improve their game; it helped quite a bit. Many tennis players learn to juggle so that they can see the ball coming quicker and easier and to help them with their reflexes. Juggling is a sport at which men and women can be equally adept; each individual can advance at his or her own speed. Many sports seem to be seasonal, but it would be just as beneficial to practice a little juggling at home anytime.

Furthermore, juggling is a pastime you can enjoy alone or with partners, and you can do it almost anywhere, any time. That's one of the beauties of it. The equipment is portable and constitutes all that you need for practice and performance. On your lunch hour at work, for instance, juggle for half an hour. It will leave you feeling refreshed and able to return to work in a happier frame of mind in which to get more accomplished.

Another thing: you are never too old to begin. You do not have to be a youngster to succeed in learning to juggle. I know of one juggler who was 27 years old when he began, and he went on to have a fantastic professional career. I have also heard of people that were 70 years old that learned to juggle (yes, you can teach an old dog new tricks). Neither is anyone too young to take up juggling. Anthony Gatto started juggling at the age of 5. Guided by his father Nick, Anthony went on to become one of the best jugglers in the world by the age of 11. When Anthony came to see my act while I was performing in Atlantic City, I could tell that he really wanted to be on that stage, and in a few years he was performing his great act in Las Vegas. Anthony is still young and who knows how far he will go.

The young Anthony Gatto.

It's easy to get a youngster interested. Simply have her toss a ball straight up above her head and then you catch it. Make sure she throws the ball in a straight line up to your hand. Next, have her throw the ball from hand to hand on her own. Young or old, after this simple beginning the learner is on his way. Younger people have a short attention span, so allowance must be made for that. But attention span aside, once the spark of interest has been struck, all anyone needs is to follow the easy directions on how to learn juggling found in this book, and he or she can go as far as time and patience permits.

Juggling is exclusively a human talent. No other animals have been able to learn to juggle 3 objects (although I have known some human jugglers that were animals). I am sure that you would get rich if you could teach a monkey to juggle more than 2 objects and perform. That juggling is unique to humans should not be surprising since it involves not only remarkable use of the hands, but also complex spatial perception and cognitive skills.

The basic pattern for juggling, and for most of the tricks that I describe, is called the cascade. The cascade pattern is used when doing an odd number of objects: 3,5,7,9,87 etc. Please see Chapter Two, How to Begin to Juggle, to learn the 3 ball cascade pattern. The main force acting on juggling when you are on the earth is gravity, although air resistance is also a factor. You cannot overcome gravity, unless you juggle in outer space, so you have to learn to use it to your advantage.

KiT
Keep Look-
ing Up

Paul

July 9, 1891

MR. B - PRINCE OF JUGGLERS

Doing a 3 ball cascade, Paul Bachman.

The record number of objects that I have seen or heard of being juggled are 10 balls, 11 rings, 7 clubs, 8 plates, 5 cigar boxes, 8 sticks, 5 hats, or 7 ping-pong balls. But don't conceive these to be limits to what you can accomplish. As far as I know juggling is limitless. Your imagination is the only limit. For hundreds of centuries, in one way or another, people have attempted to defy gravity. For numbers, PRACTICE and the power of POSITIVE THINKING pays off. Think little goals and expect little achievements; think big goals and achieve big success. When you believe you can do something, your mind finds ways to do it. But don't think that you have to juggle a large number of objects to have fun with juggling. You can also have a great time with 3 objects. When performing, easier tricks done with a lot of style and showmanship go over much better than a trick done sloppily and uncaringly. Hard tricks or numbers done with a great deal of style can be even more impressive.

With 5 clubs, Manuel Zuniga.

There are endless possibilities of props that can be juggled and tricks that can be done. You will learn in time that trying to throw ever more objects by tossing them higher increases the inaccuracy of each throw but does not buy a proportional amount of time. Throw a prop twice as high and it stays aloft about forty percent longer. To get twice as much time for catching, you will need to throw a prop four times as high. An 11 ring cascade stretches toward the limit of the juggler's duel with gravity. A ring that is thrown 15 feet high, for example, takes 3½ seconds to leave the hand and return again. But throwing a ring 30 feet in the air, as must be done in juggling 11 rings, produces only 5 seconds of flight time. So the net gain from doubling the height of a 3½ second throw is only about 1½ seconds. The addition of more props demands incredible precision. A tiny deviation in timing or aim will cause a numbers act to literally collapse into a floor show.

The world has seen many great numbers jugglers. One of the first who was documented was the Italian Enrico Rastelli (1896-1931). Rastelli often juggled an even number of objects throwing in pairs. He managed to juggle 10 balls throwing pairs although he could not cascade 9 balls. Rastelli elevated juggling to a much higher level; he is to jugglers what Caruso is to tenors. His many feats included juggling either 10 balls, 8 plates, or 8 sticks. He could also bounce 3 medium-sized balls on his head. Rastelli performed in the United States a few times, one of which was at the Hippodrome in New York in 1923. Unfortunately, Rastelli died from an infection in his mouth caused by a mouthstick, which is a stick that is held in the mouth and is used to manipulate props. Rastelli died at such a young age, who knows how far he could have gone with juggling.

Rings are generally considered the easiest object to juggle in large numbers because they are thinner and have less chance of collision. Thus you can hold more of them in your hands. Sergei Ignatov toured the United States on two occasions. He performed 11 rings a few different times while he was here. He would start 9 rings out of his hands. When he established the pattern he would throw the 9 rings a bit higher, then grab 1 more ring with each hand from a holster around his waist. It is reported that he is working on juggling 13 rings.

Clubs are considered about the hardest props to juggle in large numbers because they have to be flipped and caught by the handle. I worked on juggling 7 clubs for about a year prior to the accident in 1982. The greatest number of throws that I got with the 7 was thirty. I worked on 7 clubs because I wanted to be different. Only one person in the United States was working on it: Demetrius Alcarese.

Many of the ticks that I describe in this book can be done with any prop or combination of props. You may have to modify the trick to fit your prop — and as you become more adept and inventive, you may even modify props to fit the trick you have in mind. Anything that can be juggled, spun, balanced or manipulated in an appropriate manner can be so employed while you operate similarly or even differently with some other object. It is good practice to try any number of different props for each trick explained in this book. Of course, I can describe just a sampling of the tricks you could do, from among the standard ones already established. When you have familiarized yourself with these and attained sufficient skill through practice, you can use your imagination to find new props to use and devise new tricks at which to try your hand — or, more likely, hands!

Though anyone can do it, only a small percentage of people actually learn to juggle. So come on, become one of the lucky few, and follow me into the wonderful world of juggling. You will amaze and impress your friends; and who knows? You may even amaze yourself.

TWO
HOW TO BEGIN TO JUGGLE

So you want to learn how to juggle. If you don't already know how to juggle, this chapter will let you in on the secret. Once you learn how to juggle, you do not have to become an expert with balls before you move on to other things like clubs and rings. The following instructions are excellent for learning either of these props. With the clubs you use a single flip as it is thrown. For rings you have to spin the ring out of your hand as it is released. If you already know how to juggle, this is a good system to use to teach someone else. I have taught many people to juggle in 15 to 20 minutes using this method. Heavier balls such as lacrosse balls or bean bags are the best to juggle with, since they tend to land in your hand and stay there.

• THE THREE KEYS TO JUGGLING IN A CASCADE •
---

1 BALL   It is best to be standing up so that you can maneuver well to catch the ball. If you stand over a bed you will not have to reach down very far to retrieve a dropped ball. Throw one ball to the other hand at about six inches above your head. Throw the ball back and forth to the same center point. Do not watch the ball the whole time as it is traveling to the other hand. Watch the top of its arc as it is thrown. Do not watch the ball land in your hand.

2 BALLS   Have one ball in each hand. Throw one ball to your other hand and when it reaches its apex, throw the other ball up the same height as the first ball, so that it lands in the hand that threw the first ball. The paths of the balls should cross at a center point, the second ball going underneath and to the inside of the first ball. Start with the same hand throwing first every time for a while. Then practice using the other hand throwing first every time for a while. Finally switch off the lead hand each time you throw.

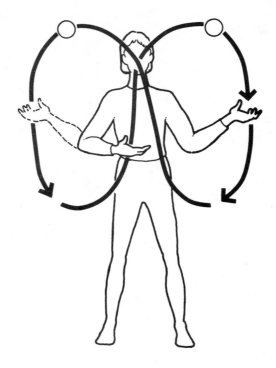

3 BALLS   Have 2 balls in preferred hand and one ball in the other hand. Start with the hand with 2 balls in it. At first just do two throws, one from each hand. Hold the third ball without releasing it. For 3 balls, start throwing as you did using 2 balls. When the second ball is coming down, throw the third ball up under the second ball thrown. Then do the same thing with the other hand, and back and forth. Now you are juggling! Always throw from the inside and catch on the outside. From the front, the pattern you are doing should look like a figure eight. Also practice starting with your non-dominant hand.

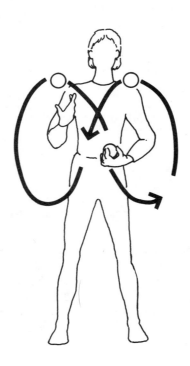

Keep your forearms parallel to the floor with your hands about shoulder width apart. Your throws will go at approximately a 60 degree angle as the ball is thrown to the other hand. All of your throws have to be at the same height and angle. It helps to think of two imaginary points about 12 inches above each hand at which to aim. Before you begin, learn to move your arms up, and down in rhythm without releasing the balls. Count 1-2, 1-2, to work on the timing of the juggling. If you tend to throw out too far forward, try standing in front of a wall while you juggle. Once you smack into the wall a few times you will stop throwing too far forward very quickly. Really, the fear of running into the wall will teach you to throw the balls up straight, instead of forward. You should concentrate more on the catch than the throw. The throw will come naturally. Seen from the front, your hand should throw from the center and catch on the outside. Seen from the side, your pattern must not vary much from front to back. Do not go too fast with your juggling. One throw at a time. Many people tend to go too quickly when learning to juggle.

When catching a ball that is coming down, your hand should close lightly, your fingers closing just enough to keep the ball from rolling out. W.C. Fields once said, "Don't hang on to what you catch - just sort of boost it."

It is helpful to count your throws each round. Try to increase the number of throws each time. Everyday try to catch about 5 throws more than the day before.

As you begin to catch on to juggling 3 balls, teach someone else to juggle, because the teacher is usually the one who learns the most.

Using 3 balls, Rudy Schweitzer.

Once you can juggle 3 balls or clubs, work on varying the height of the pattern. Juggle in a high pattern and also a low pattern. Try looking at something in front of you while you are juggling (and avoid looking so much at the props). Next try walking and juggling. Finally work on juggling while walking and looking at something other than the props.

It is well to begin with a trick that isn't too hard, such as an under the leg throw; juggling in a high pattern; or 1 up 2 up, where you throw 1 ball up out of the pattern, then the 2 other balls thrown at the same time with each hand, and the 1 alone again. So that you are doing 2 balls in one hand, and 1 in the other hand.

If you can juggle 3 balls and want to learn 3 rings, the understanding of the basic cascade pattern (i.e. order of throws) will transfer to rings. However, the throw and catch are different and must be learned. Note that the extent to which you get transfer effects depends upon the difficulty level of the task. As skills become more complex you will have less transfer. Thus, if you can juggle 5 rings and want to do 5 clubs, you may have very little transfer effect. However, I believe the more skills that you possess, the more likely you will excel in learning due to transfer of those skills to novel situations.

Now that you are an addict (and yes, juggling is very addicting), you can spend many hours practicing and learning about the exciting juggling art.

• SUMMARY: JUGGLING IN A 3-BALL CASCADE •

— Heavier balls are best for beginning.

— Stand up while practicing.

— Throw the ball(s) from the inside, to a center point about six inches above your head, in a figure eight pattern.

— Keep your forearms parallel to the floor.

— Keep your hands shoulder width apart.

— Try to keep all throws the same height and angle.

— RELAX!

THREE
HOW AND WHERE TO PRACTICE

Now that you know how to juggle, you should practice your skills. Practicing juggling will provide many hours of real fun and enjoyment.

Juggling provides such a thrill when you learn a new trick. You will get great satisfaction when you start to accomplish your goal. But there are always new tricks to learn, and therefore, an ever expanding world of satisfaction is opened before you.

But remember, to be a good juggler will take patience, determination, and a good attitude about your juggling and yourself. Juggling will teach you to like yourself in a positive way. The only thing that you have to give up to get what you want is the idea that you cannot have it. Belief in success is the one basic, absolutely essential ingredient in a successful person. A person is a product of his own thoughts. Launch your success offensive with an honest, sincere belief that you can succeed.

If you watch children at play, you will, no doubt observe their adaptability. By this I mean that children will adapt to the "rules" of a game to suit their individual needs. For example, a group of 9- or 10-year-olds may make a special rule for a player 13 years old that will limit the older child's age advantage. In addition, children tend to use the minimum amount of structure when they play. Because grownups live in a very structured world, it is more difficult for them to "get loose." I think it is important for a juggler to be able to "play" with a trick. Adults seem to have a set way in which to do things. But it is through this medium that one "invents" new tricks. Furthermore, I think it makes you a faster learner in general. This same type of "play" is helpful to scientists, writers, etc. Learn to let yourself go occasionally.

Francis Brunn, one of the world's greatest jugglers once said, "I'm like a slave to rehearsal; it's an every day job. It's pushing my body to the absolute limit. I find time to practice every day. It's always been hard. I remember when I started, I would work so hard and fast, I'd lose my wind and my lips would turn blue. It's better now. I think that experience helps. I know how to pace myself now. What I find continually fascinating is that it's never the same. Every show is different and every rehearsal is different."

Juggler Francis Brunn.

A write-up on the great juggler Enrico Rastelli states, "Rastelli had at an early age the wise, but painful, idea that life for a person who wishes to top his forerunners can be dreadfully short. Therefore, for thirty years, he practiced from sunup to sundown; and, sunup to sundown, reminded himself that every minute and manner of life must center around the furtherance of his art. Not a moment is to be wasted, and not a moment is to be for nothing. Not only must food, rest, exercise, and women be arranged so as to help, not hurt the art. Things like weight lifting and sprinting, of course, will strain you, and should not be participated in. Rastelli often practiced twelve hours a day, and seldom less than six."

Bouncing a ball on his head and juggling 6 plates, Enrico Rastelli.

America's great juggler Bobby May once said, "Juggling is a big undertaking. It is a matter of constant practice. You may miss anytime; there is always that possiblity to worry about. I depend on a bit of ad lib to cover it gracefully. A juggler is susceptible to everything — lights, disturbances out front, his own condition. I was nervous today. That's unusual for me. Everything tells on you in time."

Bobby May.

When I was in Hawaii with the remarkable juggler, Barrett Felker, we would practice in the wrestling gym at the college. Sometimes we would practice in the day, go home and have dinner, then back to the gym to practice some more. Please don't tell them, but if the gym was locked we would climb in the window and then practice. Some nights we stayed until two in the morning. We both advanced to a higher level by putting in that much time.

Two shots of Barrett Felker.

Some people practice when they can, perform when they cannot practice, and eat and sleep when they can neither practice nor perform. I have known some people (myself included) who practice up to 12 hours a day, and then are impatient for the next day when they can practice some more. Try to work your practice time up to whatever is comfortable to you. But it is the quality of the workout, rather than the quantity, that you want to strive for. Relative emphasis can and should vary. If you are preparing for a show or a competition strive for quality; if you are learning a new trick strive for quantity.

You should have a good time when you practice; don't force yourself, which will only slow down your progress. You have to relax; then the pattern becomes easier. The novice should remember that patience is a virtue in the practice of juggling; if you are in an irritable state of mind, it is best not to attempt new feats. You will certainly fail and, worse, reinforce bad patterns or habits into your juggling.

Practicing is something that you have to work up to. It is hard to just go out and put in two or three hours of practice. Every day put in a little more time. You will find that as time goes by and you gain confidence in your juggling, your practice sessions will become longer and more enjoyable. Work your practice time up to whatever you are comfortable with. If you can get the attitude that if you miss a day, you are losing out and getting worse on the various tricks that you are learning, this will give you the incentive to practice every day. Bear in mind that repetition equals skill. Just remember to have fun and do not force yourself too much. Remind yourself regularly that you are better than you think you are. Never sell yourself short. Blend persistence with experimentation. Stay with your goal, but don't beat your head against a wall. Try new approaches. Experiment. Now don't miss out today!

Try to practice with other jugglers. Although juggling is a solo venture, it is good to have other people around to inspire and help you. Talk about your triumphs and your difficulties. Don't be afraid to ask how to do a trick; jugglers are no longer gypsies with a secret art. If you have a friend who began juggling about the same time as you, try to practice with him or her often. A friendly competition will develop and you will advance much faster. When I first began juggling, I practiced with Jon Held (now a member of the magnificent juggling group Air Jazz) everyday, and I am sure that neither of us would have reached the level we did in juggling without that friendly competition.

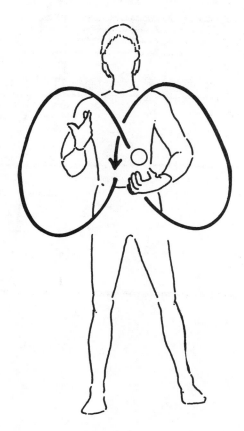

Find a good setting to practice in, such as a gym or racquetball court. Indoors you will not have to contend with the sun or the wind. You shouldn't practice on a freeway; it usually gets too windy with the traffic. Make sure that you have enough height for what you are working on and that the lighting is adequate. It is good to practice over a mat to protect your props. Practicing to music adds rhythm to your juggling and makes practice sessions more fun. If you can, video tape the moves you're learning and analyze how you can improve your juggling. Juggling in front of a mirror can also help. Don't always practice in the same place; choose several places. In each place you will have a different atmosphere, lighting, background, etc. Learn to juggle under any circumstance. But when first learning a new move, practice in the place that you usually practice in. A frameless backpack is good for carrying your juggling props when you go practice. That way you have your arrns free in case you have to carry something else. It is also more comfortable.

(drawing by Peter Davison)

Before you practice it is beneficial to do a good stretch out. To juggle well you really must be loose. Stretch your whole body, upper and lower. Try to be very limber. This will increase the blood flow to the arms and help fine tune the reflex systems. I also include a good stretch at the end of my practices to keep the muscles loose.

In my practice sessions, I would do a good stretch of my entire body to begin with. After I did the stretch I had a certain warm-up routine with 3 clubs that I had to complete before I went on with the rest of my practice. When I got to the point in which I could usually complete this warm-up in the first try, I would add more tricks to make it more difficult. After I did the warm-up routine, I would work on new tricks that I was learning. Finally, I practiced going over my entire show. I was very disciplined and structured in my practice sessions although I would change the procedure now and then for variation. But generally, I kept this practice routine. This may not be good for you, but it really helped me.

In your practice session, don't just work on different tricks, but use your mind to think about what your are doing wrong in performing the tricks; then figure out how they can be improved. If you keep practicing a trick incorrectly, you may eventually be unable to do the trick correctly. You don't get better by chance; you get better by change. If you drop while practicing (if you drop, that is!), do not say to yourself "Oh # ¢ & % *, I dropped," but think of it more as "Oh good, I get to try again." Then figure out why you dropped, and try not to repeat your error the next time. What you want to do is tell yourself, "I never see failure as failure, but only as a learning experience." Study setbacks to help you pave your way to success. When you make a mistake, learn, and then go back and win next time. Tell yourself, "There is a way to solve this problem," and positive thoughts rush into your mind to help you find a solution. It's believing there is a way that is important. Stop blaming luck. Research each setback. Find out what went wrong. As you are practicing, never tell yourself, "I think I'm going to drop," because you undoubtedly will. If you think that you are beaten, you are. Good juggling does not always go to the stronger or faster person, but sooner or later the person who wins is the person who thinks he can. The attitude, "Okay, I'll give it a try, but I don't think it will work" produces failures. Really believe there is no chance that you can fail. Think doubt and fail; think victory and succeed. When you believe, really believe, something can be done, your mind goes to work for you and helps you find the ways to do it. If you can mentally picture yourself doing something you want to accomplish, it helps quite a bit. Research is not conclusive, but it shows some evidence that mental practice does help, especially for routines and combinations. As you go to sleep at night, using a positive attitude, think and picture yourself doing whatever it is you want to accomplish. Tell yourself how much better you are getting at everything in life. You will be surprised at how much this can help. When you are having trouble doing something, much of it could be that you are telling yourself that you are having trouble. Think positive!

As you are practicing, it helps to use cue words on every throw. Such as "straight, even, straight, even." This enters your subconscious mind and reinforces the correct strategy.

Keeping a record or diary of your practice sessions is a good way to document improvements. As you are practicing, you try to reach a certain record number of throws so that you can list the accomplishment. Note what factors contribute most to your success. Review your logs from time to time and note these factors again. This is also a place where you can write comedy lines and ideas that you think of as you are practicing.

Much of what is involved in learning different tricks is learning to keep your concentration and discipline focused on whatever trick you are working. Do not let your mind drift. Concentrate on every throw and catch. Don't start thinking about the weather, Leah, or your dog, Spotty.

When learning tricks, keep your body as upright and straight as you can, but loose. Once you have learned the tricks, then you can move with the juggling. Good posture is appealing to an audience. You might also want to practice in front of a mirror to work on your posture. Sometimes people keep themselves too stiff when they juggle and it affects their juggling. Try to relax and see how you do. You might even stretch out some more. It is a good idea to take dance classes. They are good for limbering up, coordination, and movement on stage. Gymnastics can also help. Make sure that you don't keep your mouth open when you are practicing. This is a habit that many jugglers get into when learning a new trick. You might also catch a fly with your mouth open. Keep your face relaxed and natural.

It is better to try not to go too fast with your juggling. Learn a trick at a fast rate of speed and also at a slow one. Some tricks look better done at a slower rate of speed. Many times people have to learn to slow themselves down when juggling.

The lower you can keep the throws while you are juggling, the more control you will have. Try varying the height of your pattern and your eye-level as you look at the pattern. When you look higher at the pattern, you will tend to throw higher. Eyesight level does influence your pattern. If you are having trouble learning a trick, if might be where your eye level is while looking at your juggling pattern.

Practice difficult tricks at the same time that you are learning easier ones. I worked on 7 balls at the same time that I started working on 5 balls. I am sure that the 7 helped my 5, and at the same time it helped me get the feel of 7 balls. Do not think that you have to master easier tricks before moving on to more difficult things. It is only those who have gone too far who know how far they can go.

With 7 balls, Tom Dewart.

When you practice numbers, as in 5 clubs or 7 balls, count the number of throws from one of your hands. In this way you will be able to judge progress. It is easiest to just count the throws from one hand. Counting is not something that you just do. It is something that you have to teach yourself. When you practice a trick, know the number of throws that you think you can do. Then in practice, set a goal beyond this number. Keep practicing that trick until you achieve the number of throws that you are aiming for. This will help further your progress. Belief in limits creates limited people; don't put a limit on anything in your life. Set your goals high, and then exceed them. As you improve on various tricks on which your are working, increase the number of throws that your try. Bring this number up to one with which you will be happy, but realize that there are no limits to what you can accomplish.

Sometimes you have to make a trick very large for the audience to see well. Practice each trick as big and with as much movement as you can. Also learn to do the trick small and intricate. You have to make each trick very clear and definite for the audience to see well. When you are putting together a routine, try to do a very large trick, followed by a small and intricate trick. Have variety in your show.

Doing transitions from trick to trick is in itself a trick. It is something that you have to practice. You may be able to do one trick perfectly, and a different one perfectly also, but you might have trouble going from one trick to another. Don't learn one trick and then stop, and then go onto a different trick. Work on going from one trick into another, so that the tricks flow well. This will help your show look nice and smooth to the audience.

Finally, in a day of practice try to finish with an accomplishment. It is good to end the practice session with a good attitude.

• SUMMARY: HOW AND WHERE TO PRACTICE •

— Practice in a gym or enclosed area.

— Do a good stretch before practicing.

— Stay loose, relaxed; don't force yourself.

— Use your mind to figure out why you might be dropping.

— Keep your concentration and confidence.

— Have fun!

FOUR
1,2,3,4,5,6,7,8,9,10, BALLS

Ball juggling is the art of manipulating balls in a way that you appear to have a stream of balls, all racing in an orderly manner after one another, but completely under the control of the juggler. Balls do seem to be the easiest objects to juggle (although I don't know why, since they don't have a very large handle.) Games with balls have been popular since ancient times. The word ball means not only a spherical object, but an assembly for dancing. The goal of your practice is basically to teach the balls to dance.

Juggling in an orderly manner
(drawing by Peter Davison)

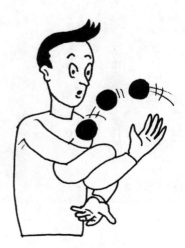

There have been many great ball jugglers. Enrico Rastelli was one of the first to be well documented. He most often juggled balls, thrown from each hand in pairs so that the balls did not cross a center point. It is reported that he juggled 10 balls, yet he could not cascade 9 balls. He could also bounce 2 balls in columns using only his head. Bobby May, one of the world's best jugglers ever, was the originator of many juggling tricks. One trick he included in his act was standing on his head and bouncing 5 balls off a drum. He was very smooth with 3 balls. He used the whole stage when he performed. One of the top ball jugglers of the 1980's is Peter Davidson. He has a style similar to Bobby May's, but still his own. A person whom I started out juggling with was Michael Baldridge. He uses tennis balls in his act. They are very lightweight, but he manages to do a superb act with the tennis balls. This shows you that it's whatever you get used to using in your juggling that matters. Michael Moshen definitely has his own style. He does things with one ball that totally amaze me. His style is very flowing and dance-like.

Manipulating 3 balls, Kris Kremo.

When I was in Hawaii juggling with the wonderful juggler, Barrett Felker, I talked with a woman from Tonga, who told me that juggling was a game on her island. Only the women participated. They would see how many balls they could shower, yes shower! (Please see glossary for definition of shower.) They would have a competition. One would bet another; she juggled until she missed then the other would take her turn. As many as 7 green tui tui nuts were showered. The women to whom I talked did not even know how to cascade 3, only how to shower them. The Los Angeles Times reported in 1978 that Nuku' alofa on the island of Tonga may have more jugglers per square mile than any other place on earth.

I like to juggle a heavier ball, such as a lacrosse ball, which is used in the game of lacrosse. Lighter balls tend to bounce out of the catching hand. With a heavier ball you really know when it lands in your hand, and it will not bounce out. Lacrosse balls can be purchased at your local sporting goods store, or from a juggling prop maker. Acetone from a hardware store is good to use to clean lacrosse balls. It cleans them off perfectly, and leaves them with an excellent grip. Currently I am using the new silicone ball that recently came out. It has a great bounce and stays clean. Silicone balls are available from most prop-makers. Although expensive, I highly recommend these balls.

You can use balls in varying sizes. Try basketballs, volleyballs, golf balls, or even shoot for the moon. When you first begin, use a heavier ball that is about the size of a tennis ball. Bean bags are good because they won't roll away when dropped.

When juggling 2 or more balls in one hand, it is best to throw them in a circle from the center to the outside. To release 3 balls out of one hand, hold one ball using the fingertips, one ball using the thumb, and the last ball with the little finger. They should be touching each other in the center. Throw the fingertip ball first, the ball held with the thumb, and the ball held with the little finger last. To start 4 balls out of one hand, hold 3 as previously explained. Then hold the fourth ball on the fingertips of the ring finger and the little finger. Release the ball held with the little finger and ring finger first. To start 5 balls out of one hand, hold 4 as I just explained. Tighten down on the ball held between your little finger and ring finger by holding it between these fingers a bit harder. Then place the fifth ball on top of the 4. Start with this ball first.

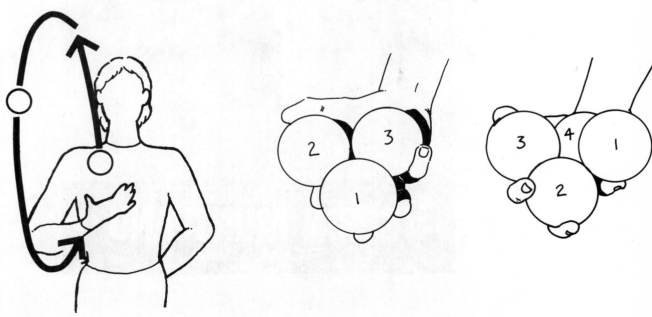

Head Bounce   You can bounce a ball on your head while juggling anything. To do this try to keep the ball low and controlled. When the ball bounces up out of line, do not bounce the ball too far in the return direction. You cannot move your body very much while you are doing this and juggling, so learn to bounce the ball well before trying to combine it with juggling. More than one ball can be bounced with the head, bouncing them so that they bounce in columns, straight up and down. For more than one ball you will have to experiment with the height of the bounces to find the right height for the number of balls that you are doing. Larger balls are the best for doing this trick.

STAR JONGLEUR
◆◈▶ **SORIN MUNTEANU** ◀◈◆
ROMÂNIA

Jack Bremlov, 6 rings while bouncing a ball on his head.

Foot Bounce   Bounce a ball back and forth, foot to foot while juggling. This is more of a catch and a throw, rather than a kick. With this trick keep the ball as low and controlled as possible. Be sure to keep your foot exactly parallel to the ground, to insure that the ball bounces up in a straight line. You don't have to lift the ball very much from one foot to the other when performing this trick.

Francis Brunn, bouncing 1 ball from foot to foot while juggling 3 balls (and jumping rope!).

Heel Kick   Hold a ball between your heels; then lift it up above your head with your feet by jumping and releasing the ball. When it comes down, keep it bouncing on your head. When doing this, try to bring your feet up as far as you can. The ball should go about 3 feet above your head before it comes down.

Arm Roll   Roll a ball from one arm to the other so that it goes behind your head. Hold the ball in one hand; throw the ball just above your hand. Have your hand a little higher than elbow height. When the ball starts rolling, bring your hand level. As the ball gets to your neck, do a neck catch (See 3 Ball Neck Catch, later in the book). Then roll the ball down the other arm and catch the ball in your hand.

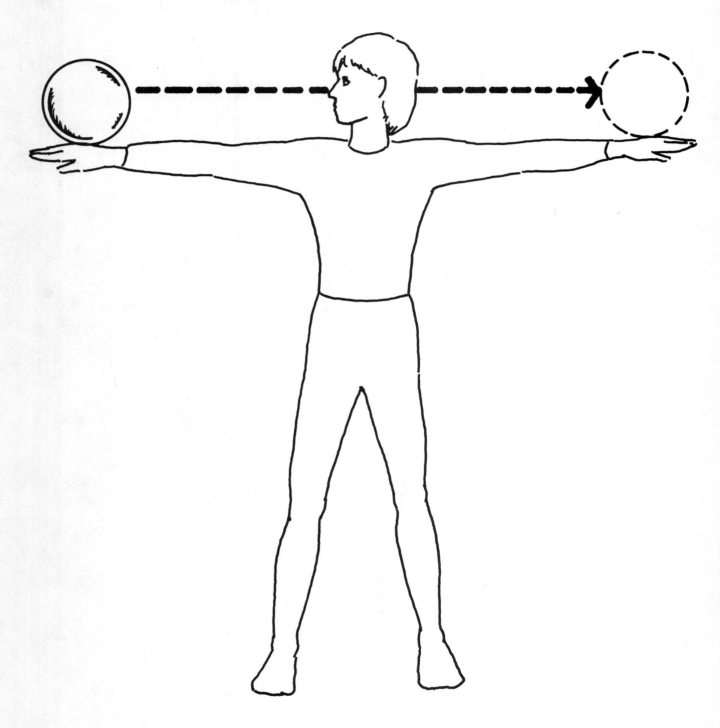

Rudy Cardenas, rolling a ball from hand to hand.

Arm Circle Roll a ball around your arms held in a circle in front of you. Keep the ball to the inside of the your arms with your fingers interlocked. To keep the ball going, you have to raise and lower your arms in time with the ball as it is traveling. The momentum of the ball rolling will keep it from falling.

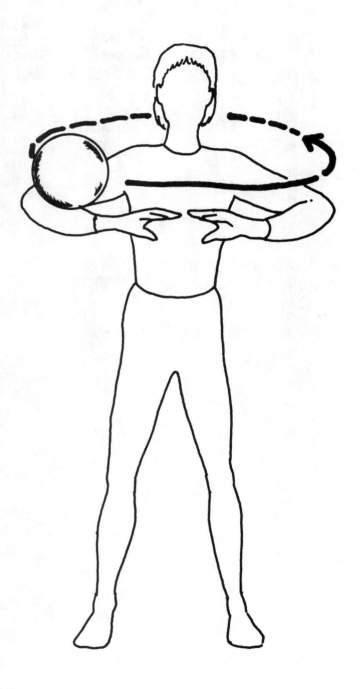

Head Roll   This is something for which Henry VIII was famous. Place a ball on your forehead with your head tilted back. You may have to wrinkle your forehead slightly to make the ball stay in place. You will still have to balance the ball to make it stay on your forehead. Now drop your head slowly to the side so that the ball rolls to your temple and stops. Roll the ball back to your forehead. Now roll the ball to your other temple. It does help to keep the ball rolling as slowly as possible. Keep your knees bent and your weight well back on your heels. It is also a great help to practice this trick in front of a mirror.

Try rolling the ball from temple to temple without stopping at the forehead. The key here is to keep the ball rolling slowly. Try to always keep the ball on a very flat plane.

Now try this: Forehead, temple, neck catch, other temple, forehead. Do this in four stages stopping at each point.

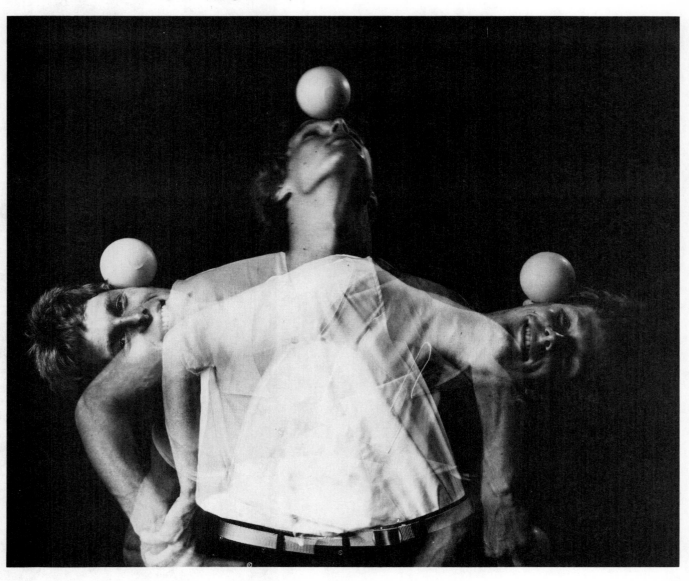

Mark Neisser doing the head roll.

Bobby May, the head roll.

Peter Scolari, in the middle of doing the head roll.

Leg Roll   Balance a ball on your foot with your leg out straight in front of you. Lift your foot slightly to start the ball rolling toward your hip. Let the ball roll up your leg and then turn away from the ball so that the ball rolls across your back toward you head. When the ball gets to your shoulder, let it continue down your arm to the back of your hand.

Francis Brunn, about to roll the ball up his leg, across his back, and to the back of his fingers.

Neck Catch   Throw 1 ball a bit higher out of a cascade. Keep watching the ball as long as you can while bending under the ball. Bring your shoulders back so that you make a 3 point pocket using your head and 2 shoulder blades as a pocket for the ball to land in. Remember that this is a catch; don't just bend forward and let the ball land. Go down at the same time as the ball is coming to your neck. Keep your face to the front the whole time you are doing this trick.

To get out of this trick, you can either roll the ball down your back and go into a juggle after catching the ball behind you , or you can let the ball roll forward and then snap you head up quickly to send the ball up in the air and go into a juggle.

Doing the neck catch (with style), Francis Brunn.

• 2 BALLS •

Juggling with 2 balls in one hand, you can do columns, outward circles, inward circles, over the shoulder, under the leg, reverse hand catch, juggle over your head, and roll off the head. As you are doing 2 balls in one hand you can also use your other hand to swing through the pattern as each ball is thrown.

Balance   Balance 1 ball on top of another ball. It helps to use larger balls when doing this, such as volleyballs. As you are balancing, move slowly when you are making a save on an object that is falling.

Head Bounce   Bounce 2 balls using only your head. When you start this trick do the first two bounces quickly, and then go into the correct timing for the height needed. Try to move with the body from the waist up. Keep a wide stance with your feet.

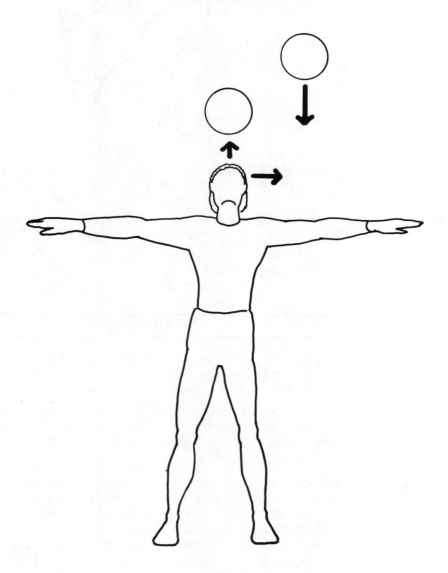

• 3 BALLS •

3 Ball Starts

To start 3 balls out of one hand, loosely hold the ball with the fingertips, one ball using the thumb, and third ball using the little finger with your palm up. The balls should be touching each other in the center. (See illustration.) Throw all 3 balls as a group. As you release the balls, flick your wrist so that the fingertip ball goes higher. After you release the balls, grab down on the 2 lower balls and go into a juggle as the last ball come down. You can do this start under your leg, behind your back, or over your shoulder.

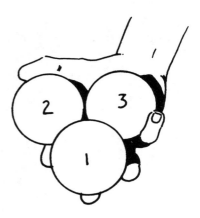

3 Behind Back, Off Head Start

Do the 3 ball start behind your back; as the last ball is coming down, let it bounce off of your head and then go into a juggle. You have to grab the 2 lower balls at about head height before the third ball bounces on your head.

Neck Catch Start

Begin with the 3 ball start behind your back, and as the last ball is coming down, do a neck catch. (See 3 ball neck catch later in this chapter.)

Heel Kick Start

Place all 3 balls between your feet, one on top of the other 2 balls. Lift all 3 balls with your feet about head high by bringing your heels up quickly together, grab down on the 2 lower balls, when the last ball comes down, go into a juggle.

• 3 BALL TRICKS •

1 Up, 2 Up

As you are doing a cascade, throw 1 ball higher, and then go into 2 balls in one hand, and 1 ball in the other hand. This trick can be done in on-sync or off-sync, although it is usually done in on-sync. (Please see glossary for definition of sync.)

Shower

For the shower, one hand makes all the throws while the other hand catches and quickly passes back to the first, so that the balls go in a circle. You can go into this from a cascade by throwing 2 balls quickly with one hand, and then start handing the balls from the other hand to the throwing hand.

3 Balls in One Hand

With 3 balls in one hand, release the first 2 balls quickly, and then fall into the rhythm for 3 balls in one hand. Remember to concentrate on the catch rather than the throw. Three balls in one hand can be done in columns, cascade, reverse cascade, shower from the inside to the outside, and shower from the outside to the inside. You can go directly into 3 balls in one hand, out of a cascade in two hands by throwing 2 balls up with the hand that you want to use for 3 in one hand. Then pass the last ball to this hand and go into 3 in one hand.

Shoulders   As you are juggling 3 balls, throw one ball over your shoulder and catch it with the other hand. For this trick you have to lift the ball in a straight line up toward the shoulder of the hand that you are throwing with, rather than going behind your back. It helps to turn your shoulder on the throwing arm toward the center as you release the ball. This trick can be done solid (please see glossary for definition of Solid) with both hands. When doing the trick solid with both hands, you always have to think of throwing the ball to a center point about one foot in front of you.

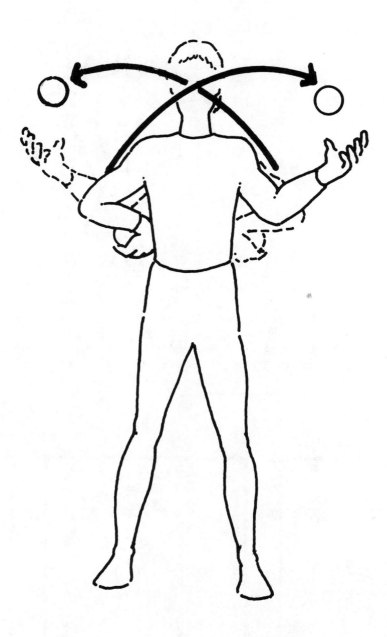

Force Bounce   Be sure to use balls that have a good bounce. Throw the balls down to the ground so that they bounce up about hand level. Throw from the outside so that they bounce up about the middle of the pattern.

Follow the Leader Bounce   Use balls that have a good bounce for this trick. Bounce 1 ball on the ground, and let it bounce a second time. As it is bouncing a second time, bounce a second ball so that it follows the first. Angle the bounce so that the ball bounces to your other hand. As you release the second ball, you have to make sure that it is in time with the first ball bounced. Don't bounce the ball too hard, just enough so that it will bounce about waist-high to your other hand. When the balls bounce over to your other hand, pass the balls back to the bouncing hand. Each ball should bounce twice before you hand it to the other hand.

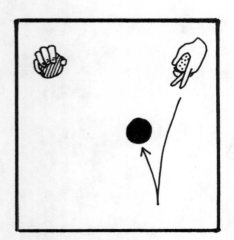  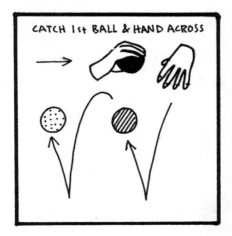

Follow the Leader Bounce (drawing by Peter Davison).

Juggle Over Head   Juggle with your hands directly over your head. Out of a cascade, throw 1 ball a little above your head and then bring your hands immediately above your head and juggle. When doing this trick, use your whole arm rather than your wrist to push the ball up.

The author juggling 3 balls over his head.

Juggle Over Head, Then Lie Down   Juggle over your head as I just explained, then as you are doing this, bend one leg under you and lie down still maintaining the juggle over your head. Then get back up the same way. Do this trick very slowly.

On-side Juggle   Juggle with both hands on one side of your body, one arm going behind your back. To get into this procedure from a cascade throw one ball a little higher and to the side. While it is in the air, quickly bring your hand behind your back and go into a juggle as the ball comes down. Keep your hips well forward for this trick and your weight on your heels. You will not be able to maneuver the hand that is behind your back very well, so make sure that the throws coming up from the other hand are very precise. Either side can be used to juggle in this manner.

Juggling 3 balls on the side, Kit Summers.

Béla Kremo

Blind In Front   Juggle without looking at the balls in front of your body by looking forward or straight up. Keep your pattern low and controlled. Try to use your wrists to juggle. Remember that juggling is more feeling than sight.

Blind Behind Back   Juggle behind your back while looking forward or above. For this trick, keep your pattern low for control. Use more arm rather than wrist to juggle behind your back. Another way to do this is to roll the balls off your back.

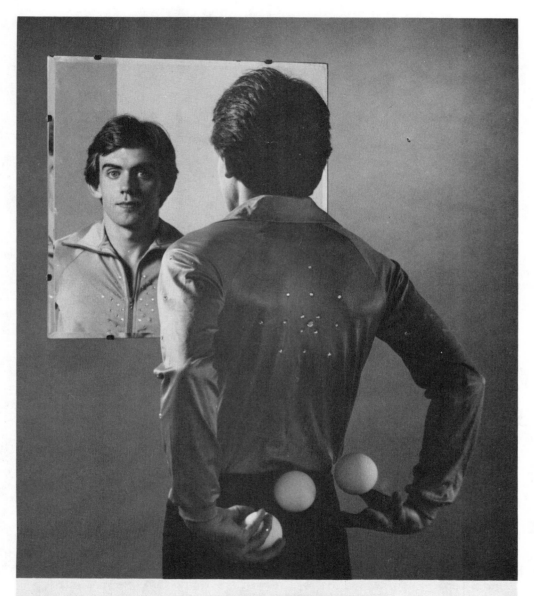

ALAN HOWARD

Cross to Other Side Behind Back   Juggle on the side of your body (see on-side juggle); then as you are doing this, go directly into the blind-behind-back juggle. Next go into the behind-back juggle on the other side. Go slowly to have more control. Lean back and bring your hips forward so that your have room to maneuver your arms.

Water Faucet   The balls go in a triangle pattern with one hand about head-high. With this pattern you have one hand about head-high and near the same shoulder, and you throw the ball up to it. After the ball is caught, you bring your hand with the ball in a straight line over to a point directly above your other hand. Then drop the ball straight down to your first hand before it is thrown up to the hand that is at head level.

(drawing by Peter Davison)

3 Ball Finishes   One way to finish with 3 balls is to pass one ball to the other hand while the third ball is in the air. Then use the empty hand to catch the last ball in the air.

Behind Back   Throw one ball a little higher and to the side. Hand 1 of the balls to your other hand, and reach behind your back with the empty hand to catch the first ball thrown.

Kneel Down, Catch Under Leg   Throw one ball a little higher and hand 1 ball to your other hand. As the ball thrown into the air is coming down, kneel on one knee, put your hand under the knee that's up, and catch the last ball in this hand.

Last Ball Lift Hat   When wearing a hat, throw 1 ball high; when it comes down, let it bounce on the ground. As it bounces up, lift your hat off your head a little, and let the ball bounce up into the hat. As the ball is under your hat, set the hat back on your head without turning the hat upside down.

• 4 BALLS •

Usually 4 balls are juggled in a fountain a pattern. First work on juggling 2 balls in one hand in a circle from the inside to the outside. Throw the balls about three inches above your head. Concentrate on the catch rather than the throw. Then work on the other 2 balls in the other hand. You do not have to master juggling 2 balls in one hand before trying 4 balls. When learning 4 balls, juggle them off sync. Keep your hands low and do not reach up for the balls. When you are starting to get 4 balls in off sync, work on juggling 4 balls is on sync. Next try, juggling off sync, as you are juggling go into on sync, then go back into off sync. With 4 balls you really have to concentrate on keeping the two sides separate. It helps to think of a wall in between your hands, and try not to hit the wall.

• 4 BALL STARTS •

2 Behind Back

Throw 2 balls behind your back, and when they come down go directly into on sync. Even harder is to throw 2 balls behind your back, then throw the other 2 balls behind your back on the other side, and go immediately into a 4 ball spread (see glossary for the explanation of a spread).

ehind Back or Under Leg

Throw all 4 balls behind your back or under your leg, grab down on 2 balls, and go directly into on sync.

• 4 BALL TRICKS •

Shower

To go into the 4 ball shower, start holding 2 balls in each hand. Throw the 2 out of one hand, 1 at a time, about four feet in the air, then pass one ball from the other hand to the showering hand and go into a shower. To start while juggling 2 balls in each hand, quickly throw 2 balls high out of the hand with which you want to shower, about four feet in the air; while you do this hold the 2 in the other hand and pass these balls to the showering hand one at a time and go into a shower.

Shower, Throw 1 High

As you are doing the 4 ball shower, throw 1 ball high and shower the other 3 balls for two throws. As the ball comes down, go back into a shower. You have to experiment with the height of the 1 ball thrown high to get the right timing to go back into a shower.

Over Head

Juggle 4 balls off sync, then throw 2 balls high, one from each hand, and go directly into 4 balls over your head. (It might help to look under 3 Balls Juggling Over Your Head.) Work on 2 balls in one hand over your head, then 2 balls in the other hand alone. For this trick your have to really use your arms, rather than your wrists to push the balls up above your head. Concentrate on keeping each side of the pattern separate.

Shoulders

As you are juggling 4 balls, throw the balls over your shoulders. First, practice juggling 2 balls in one hand throwing one ball over your shoulder. Then work on throwing shoulder throws using the other hand. You really have to concentrate on keeping your throws to the outside. Think of this trick more as a over-the-elbow-throw. Now work on juggling all 4 balls and throwing a shoulder throw. Finally, work on making shoulder throws solid with both hands. Turn your shoulder in on the throwing arm each throw.

Follow the Leader Bounce

See Follow the Leader Bounce under 3 balls. With 4 balls, each ball bounces three times instead of two.

• 5 BALLS •

First, start with only 3 balls in one hand; throw the balls to the other hand, and catch them in this hand. Next, work on throwing the balls from the starting hand to the second hand; with this hand, immediately throw the balls back to the first hand. Keep them going continuously in this manner. Basically you are juggling 3 balls in a 5 ball pattern. Now with 5 balls, attempt to flash (see glossary) 5 balls and catch them. Then try to do more than 5 throws. Do not limit yourself by telling yourself that you can't do it. After you are starting to get the 5 balls, work on juggling in a low pattern, and a very high pattern. This helps in learning control.

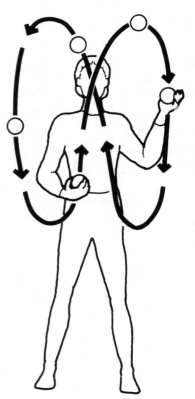

ALAN HOWARD

Half Shower   Relax the throws from one hand and throw a bit harder with the other hand so that the balls go over the top of the pattern. Concentrate more on the throws that are going over the top. It helps to turn your shoulders slightly toward the hand that is throwing over the top.

Shower   To start a 5 ball shower, have 2 balls in the throwing hand and 3 in the passing hand. Throw the first 2 balls quickly, one at a time and start passing the other balls over to the throwing hand and go into a shower. When doing a shower, pick a point above the catching hand to aim for. You can also go into a 5 ball shower from a cascade by quickly throwing from the inside of the pattern and going into a shower as the balls come down. Do the 5 ball shower in either direction.

Half Shower to Shower   Do a half-shower. Then start throwing the lower throws lower and the higher throws higher. Keep going with this until you go into a shower. For this trick relax with the half shower and start to tense your arms while you go into the shower. Take it slowly when going from the half shower to the shower.

Pairs   As you are doing a 5 ball shower, retain 2 balls with the throwing hand and throw these balls as a pair. Use your wrist to make the ball in your fingertips go higher. As the balls come down, catch them individually as in a shower. This trick can be done solid by throwing pairs out of the showering hand everytime.

Statue of Liberty   As you are doing a half shower, lift above your head the hand that is making the lower throws. You have to relax the throws from the hand that is above your head. Go into this trick slowly.

(drawing by Peter Davison)

Over Head	Juggle 5 balls over head by throwing 3 balls higher out of a cascade and quickly bring your hands above your head and go into juggling 5 balls above your head. You push the balls up using your arms more than your wrists.
Neck Catch	First go back and review the neck catch using 3 balls. For a 5 ball neck catch, throw 1 ball out of the pattern a bit higher. As the ball is in the air, catch 2 balls in each hand and then do a neck catch. To get out of the neck catch, flip the ball that's on the back of your neck up about four feet. When it comes down, go back into a cascade, or a 3 ball juggle holding the other balls in your hands before going into the 5 ball cascade.
Shoulder One	As you are juggling 5 balls in a cascade, throw 1 ball over your shoulder the same height as your 5 ball pattern. For this trick, turn your shoulder away from the hand that is throwing over your shoulder. This trick can be done solid from the one hand.
Shoulder Two	Throw solid from both hands over both shoulders. Concentrate on throwing to a center point in front of you about six inches above your head. Turn the shoulder making the shoulder throw in as you are making the throw. You will have to make your throws a bit higher than your normal 5 ball pattern.

Dana Tison, 5 ball juggling.

5 Up Pirouette,
Half Pirouette

Do a pirouette by throwing 3 balls and holding the other 2 balls as you turn, or throw all 5 balls and pirouette. For a 5 ball pirouette you will have to juggle in a low pattern and quickly throw all 5 balls up higher at one time. Turn your body slightly toward the direction that you are going to pirouette before doing the pirouette. It helps to throw the lst ball a bit higher than the other balls before you turn.

1 Up, 4 Up and Variations

Go back and review 1 up, 2 up with 3 balls at this point. For 1 up, 4 up with 5 balls you have to practice juggling 3 balls in one hand throwing a single ball and a pair of balls as one, so that you are basically juggling 2 balls in one hand. With the other hand, you throw 2 balls as one ball. You do the 5 balls like 1 up, 2 up using this technique. 5 balls can also be juggled in a cascade using this method. Juggling of this sort is called multiplex. You can use multiplex in doing many of the 3 ball tricks that are in this book.

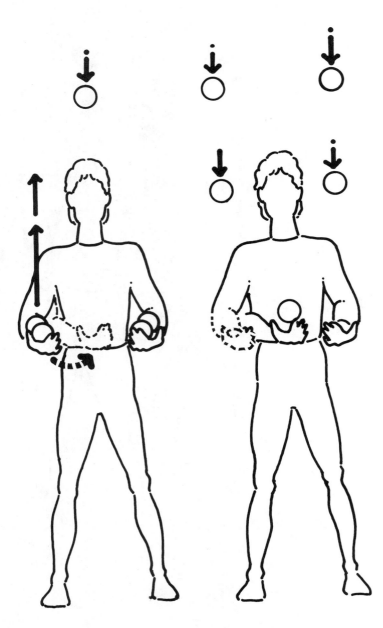

• 6 BALLS •

Work on 3 balls in each hand throwing from the inside to the outside. You don't have to be a master of 3 balls in each hand before moving on to 6 balls. You may have to practice extra hard with the hand that is not your favored hand. Work on juggling on-sync and off-sync with the 6; although for me, off-sync was easier for 6 balls.

Cross Pattern   Throw the balls on-sync crossing the pattern at a center point going to the other hand. You will have to throw one side sooner and a little higher so that the balls do not hit in the center.

Half Shower   To go directly into a half shower using 6 balls, throw on sync with both hands, after you throw the first 2 pairs of balls, start to change to off-sync timing.

6 Ball Spread   Do a spread throwing 3 different pairs of balls in front of you in three different columns. Or have two different columns and throw one pair into the first column, and then a second pair into the second column. The third pair is thrown into the first column, and back and forth.

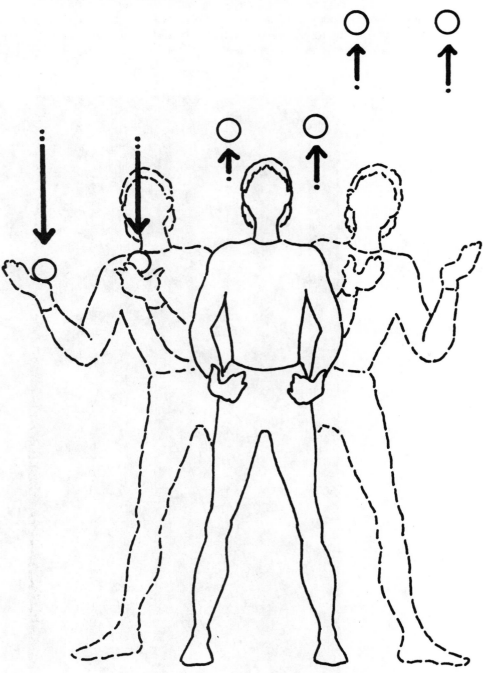

For juggling 7 balls, release the first 7 balls quickly in a cascade and then fall into timing for 7 balls. 7 balls can be juggled in a cascade, half shower, reverse cascade, and a shower.

Rudy Horn hadn't juggled in three years when I visited him in Berchtesgaden, Germany. I asked him if I could film him doing part of his act. He agreed, but added, that he might be a little rusty. One of the things he did was juggle 7 balls. He didn't seem to have any trouble, even after three years. This shows you what level you too can reach.

Juggling 7 balls, Bob Rosenberg.

• 8 BALLS •

Work on 4 balls in each hand before trying 8. The most common pattern in which to juggle 8 balls is using the center cross pattern explained under 6 balls. Release 4 balls out of one hand as explained in the introduction. You will have to experiment with the height of the pattern to find one that is right for doing 8 balls.

• 9 BALLS •

Hold 4 balls in one hand as I explained before. Hold the fourth ball between your ring finger and your little finger a bit harder, place the fifth ball on top of the 4 balls. Try to keep your pattern as narrow as possible.

A few people have managed to cascade 9 balls. Massimiliano Truzzi is said to have performed it regularly in his act.

Susan Kirby, the amazing 9 ball juggle.

Albert Lucas, throwing 9 balls.

• 10 BALLS •

The most common pattern that I have heard of for juggling 8 balls is the center cross pattern. I would think that this would be the best pattern to use to juggle 10 balls. While doing the cross pattern with 10 balls, try to cross the balls at a point about seven feet above the hands. It might help to practice doing 5 balls in one hand for a while before throwing the 10.

• SUMMARY: JUGGLING WITH BALLS •

— Use a ball with which you are comfortable. I personally like to use a heavier ball, such as a lacrosse ball.

— Keep everything smooth and flowing.

— Don't keep your pattern too narrow. Try and keep everything open enough for what you are working on.

— Keep your basic cascade pattern on a flat vertical plane in front of you.

FIVE
4,5,6,7,8,9,10,11,12,13 RINGS

Rings have less chance of collision than balls and clubs because they are thinner. Therefore, a greater number of rings can be juggled as well as held. Rings should be thrown and caught so as to be perpendicular to your shoulders. When juggling rings, your palms should be facing each other. The rings will be caught at shoulder level. To hold and start rings, hold 1 ring in your hand, laying it across your fingers. Put your little finger in between the second ring and first ring. To release more rings out of one hand, put one finger in between each ring going toward your index finger. Release the rings going form the index finger toward the little finger. To start 5 rings out of one hand, hold 4 as just explained; the fifth ring is held between the thumb and forefinger. A sixth ring can also be squeezed in about half an inch from the fifth ring. When doing any number of rings, you can finish by pulling each ring over your head using each hand. Some people tape their hands to protect them against cuts from their rings. You will have trouble juggling rings in the wind. Or, if you are juggling indoors, watch the air conditioning.

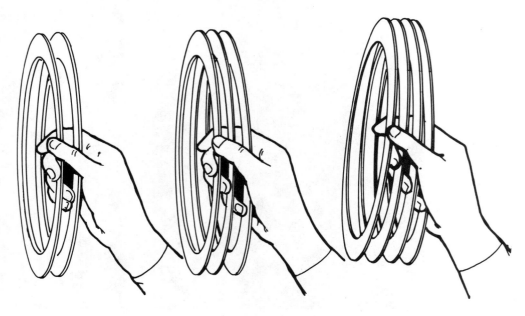

How to start rings.

Sergei Igantov, with the Moscow Circus, started juggling at the age of sixteen in Russia. The second time that he toured the U.S., he included the juggling of 11 rings in his act a number of times. Ignatov learned his juggling from Alexander and Violeta Kiss at the Moscow Circus School. Alexander, who toured the U.S. in 1963, is Sergei's idol. Ignatov considers Kiss to be the greatest living juggler. Ignatov makes his own juggling props. Albert Piotrowski is the only other juggler who I know of, at this time, who performs 11 rings. Piotrowski also does 10 rings while maintaining a head balance. Dick Franco has put many, many hours of practice into juggling with rings. It has paid off: he is one of the great ring jugglers of the world. He has come up with many of his own moves with rings which he includes in his act.

Ron Meyers, juggling 5 rings while sideways and facing the audience.

For 4 rings, juggle 2 in each hand, using outward circles in an off sync pattern. Practice 2 in one hand in each hand for a while.

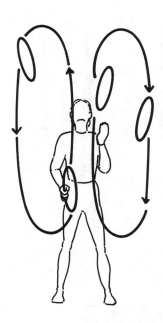 

Flat Half Shower   As you are doing a half shower, throw the rings flat (see glossary) from one hand over the top. Each throw should be thrown over the top slightly behind the preceeding throw.

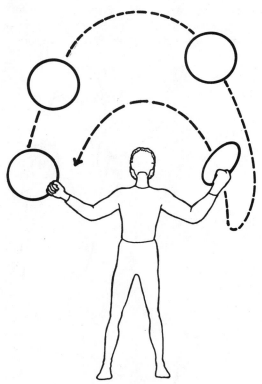

Spread   With rings, you can keep each side of the pattern very narrow, so with a ring spread, you can keep the pattern very tight and controlled. You can also stretch the pattern very wide.

Try to keep the rings as low as possible. When handling the ring across from hand to hand, you have to be very accurate, as it is easy to miss the ring.

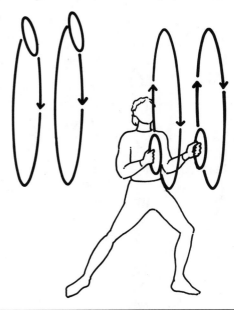

• FIVE RINGS •

First work on releasing 3 rings out of the hand that you are going to start the pattern with. Then work on keeping 3 rings going in a 5 ring pattern by starting 3 rings out of one hand and immediately throwing them back to this hand again after they are caught with the other hand. Next work on flashing 5 rings and catching them. Finally work on juggling 5 rings. Try to increase the number of throws each try.

Flat Half Shower   With one hand, throw over the top of the pattern so that your throws are parallel to your shoulders. Try not to turn your body when you are doing this. Both hands should throw at approximately the same height; the flat throws should go behind the other throws.

Flat Full Reverse   Do a full reverse cascade with flat throws. Don't concentrate too hard on getting the throws in front or behind the throw that is coming. Try to keep your throws straight above you, catching each ring on each side of your body.

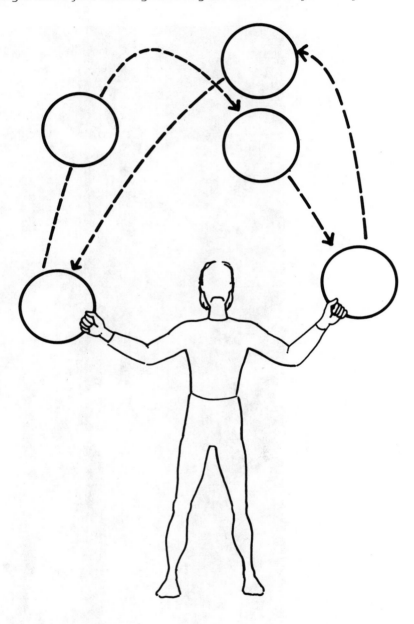

Pancakes   As you are doing a cascade, start throwing all of the throws so that they are flipped like a club rather than spun out of the hand. To go into this you will have to start doing your 5 ring cascade very wide to give you room. First work on throwing pancakes with just one hand. Then work on the other hand alone. It doesn't really matter how many flips are thrown with the rings.

Sergei Ignatov throwing pancake throws.

Back Crosses

First please refer to backcrosses with clubs. With the rings you will have to bring the ring down to your hip with the throwing arm almost straight. Then bring the ring straight up and release it. First work on 3, when you start to get the feel of this, throw 1 back throw out of a 5 ring cascade. You will really have to lift the rings from your rear end when doing this trick. I actually have not seen this trick performed before with 5, but I have practiced it myself and I am sure that it can be accomplished.

**Balance 1 on Forehead;
Juggle 4**

Before you begin to juggle, place a ring on your forehead so that it is at a right angle to your shoulders. Balance the ring on your forehead and juggle the other 4. While balancing the ring you will have to make your throws very accurate because you cannot maneuver very well. To get out of this, throw the 4 rings in a 5 ring pattern, grab the one ring off your forehead, and go into a 5 ring cascade.

Balancing 1 ring on his forehead while juggling 4 more, Ron Meyers.

Pirouette, Half Pirouette Using 3-5

Throw all 5 rings, or throw 3 and hold the other 2, and do a pirouette or a half pirouette. The rings do not have to be thrown very high when throwing them up for either of these tricks because the rings can be caught very high or very low.

Dick Bird Finish

As you are juggling 5 rings, bring 1 ring over your head, then a second ring over your head with the other hand. Flip 1 ring in a pancake throw with the hand that you used to begin putting the rings over your head. Place the other 2 rings over your head before you catch the pancake throw over your head. So it's slap, slap (over your head), flip, slap, slap, catch.

• 6 RINGS •

With 6 rings you throw in outward circles. Work on juggling 3 in each hand in outward circles, columns, and cascade pattern just so that you can learn control with 3 rings in one hand. Now work on 6 rings in off-sync and on-sync. Next work on going from off sync into sync and then back again to off sync.

ALAN HOWARD

4 Up, 6 Up Pirouette

Juggle in an on sync pattern. Then throw all 6, or hold 2 rings and throw 4, and pirouette. The rings do not have to be thrown very much higher for the pirouette. A pirouette can also be done out of an off-sync pattern, although it is harder.

Over Head, Juggle 5, Back to 6

As you are juggling 6 rings in off sync, place 1 ring over your head and start throwing the other 5 rings in a 5 ring pattern. Then go into juggling 3 rings in one hand, and 2 in the other and as the space comes around in the hand where you are juggling 2 rings, pull the ring that is over your head off and go back into juggling 6 rings.

• 7 RINGS •

Work on juggling 5 rings in a high pattern. Now work on juggling 5 rings in a high pattern using the timing that you would need for juggling 7 rings. Now work on the release you will need for 4 rings out of one hand. Just use 4 rings and throw them from your starting hand to the other hand. For 7 rings you have to make the first 7 throws quickly and then fall into the timing for 7 rings. Remember to count your throws from one hand so that you can judge improvement.

In his act, Sergei Ignatov did a wonderful routine while juggling 7 rings. Some of the tricks he included were a flat half shower, half pirouettes, full pirouettes, and pancake throws.

Half, Full Pirouettes

You do not have to throw the rings very much higher for the half or full pirouette. Try to keep the pattern narrow. It helps to count the throws as you release them, 1 through 7. Make sure that all the rings are released straight into the pattern before you turn. You can also throw 5 and hold 2 rings to pirouette.

Juggling 7 bicycle hoops, Bob Bramson.

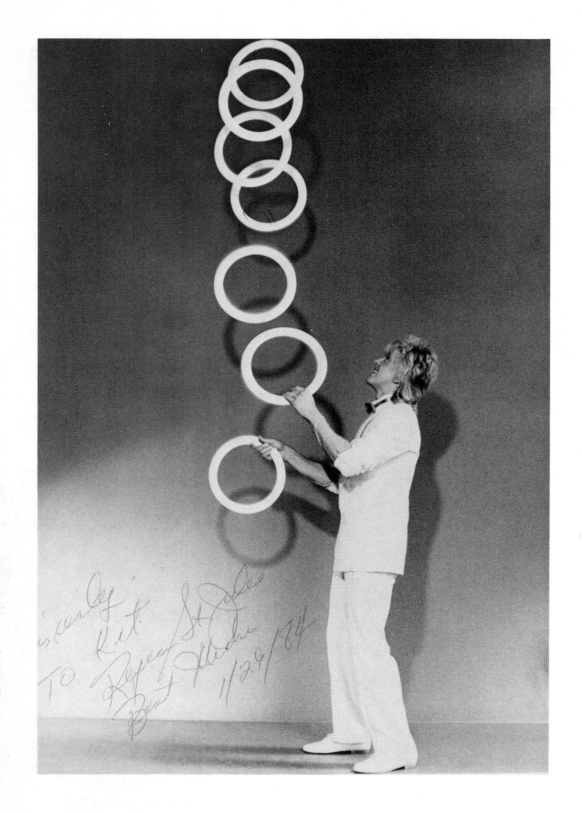

Rejean St. Jules, 7 rings.

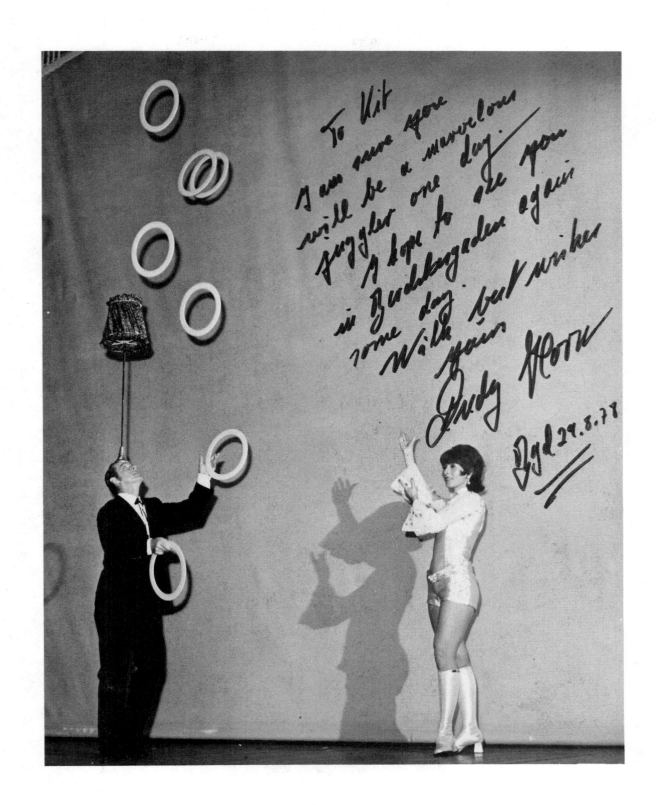

Rudy Horn, 7 rings with a balance.

For even numbers throw the rings in off sync timing in a fountain pattern. For odd numbers juggle the rings in a cascade pattern. As you increase the number of rings you will have to increase the height of the pattern. Keep the pattern as low as possible, and you will get more control. For numbers with rings you can use a ring holster. This is a belt that goes around your waist and has an attachment to hold a ring for each that you can easily grab off of the belt and send into the pattern. For 13 rings a double ring holster can be used. For numbers with rings, work on juggling 3,4, and 5 rings in one hand along with the learning of the different numbers.

8 rings with Manuel Zuniga.

Fudi, 8 ring juggle.

Rolly Brandt, 8 rings while spinning 1 on his leg.

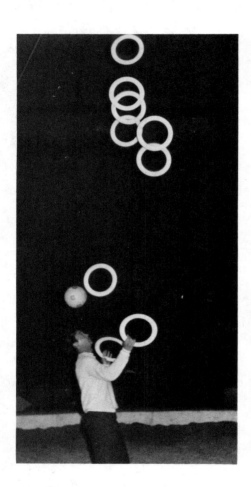

Tindra Merbs, 9 rings.

9 rings while bouncing a ball
on his head, Albert Petrowski.

10 rings in the gym, Albert Lucas.

Albert Petrowski, the incredible 11 ring juggle.

• SUMMARY: JUGGLING WITH RINGS •

— The start is very important when doing rings.

— Make sure you have a solid grip on the ring before releasing it.

— Throw and catch rings about shoulder height and in about the same place.

— Keep your eye level high.

— Tilt your head back to see the top of the pattern.

SIX
CLUBS

Juggling with clubs is somewhat more complicated than with balls or rings. While it is possible to begin juggling first with clubs; it will be much easier to begin with balls. When you are first beginning with the clubs, follow the directions on how to begin to juggle found earlier in this book. For juggling with clubs you use a single revolution of the club as it thrown.

Big club juggling, Harry Lind.

One of the best jugglers with clubs I've seen is Eva Vida. I met Eva Vida in 1978 when I was visiting Europe. She is an amazing club juggler. In her act she did 5 clubs. As she juggled the 5, she did five under the leg throws, first one leg, then the other. She won the Rastelli juggling competition that was held in Bergamo, Italy in 1973. Besides being a supreme juggler, she is also a wonderful person.

Under the leg with 5, Eva Vida.

Another talented club juggler is Barrett Felker. Barrett has put endless hours into practice; many of these hours have been devoted to club juggling. It has paid off: Barrett is one of the best jugglers around. I think that Barrett has, at one time or another, worked on every club juggling trick ever conceived.

There are many different types of clubs made by different manufacturers. You may have to try a few kinds before you find one that is correct for you. Preference is mainly determined by whatever you get used to using.

To hold and start clubs, hold one club between your thumb and index finger. The club should be held at about the center of the handle with the body of the club away from you and your palm up. Place a second club underneath the first club with the knob to the outside and the body toward the center, and hold it in the palm of your hand with your remaining fingers. There are various ways to hold and start clubs, but personally, I find this to be the best way.

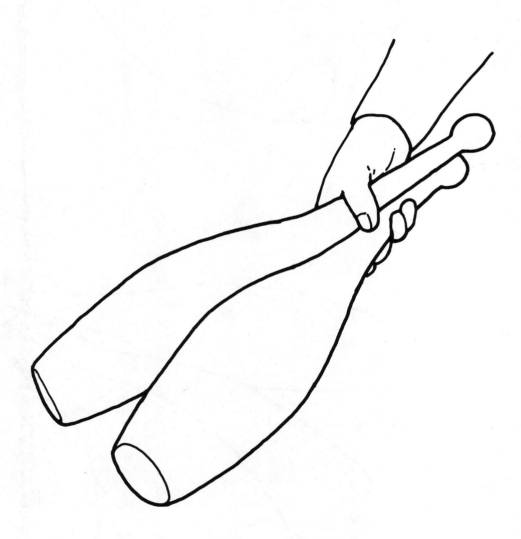

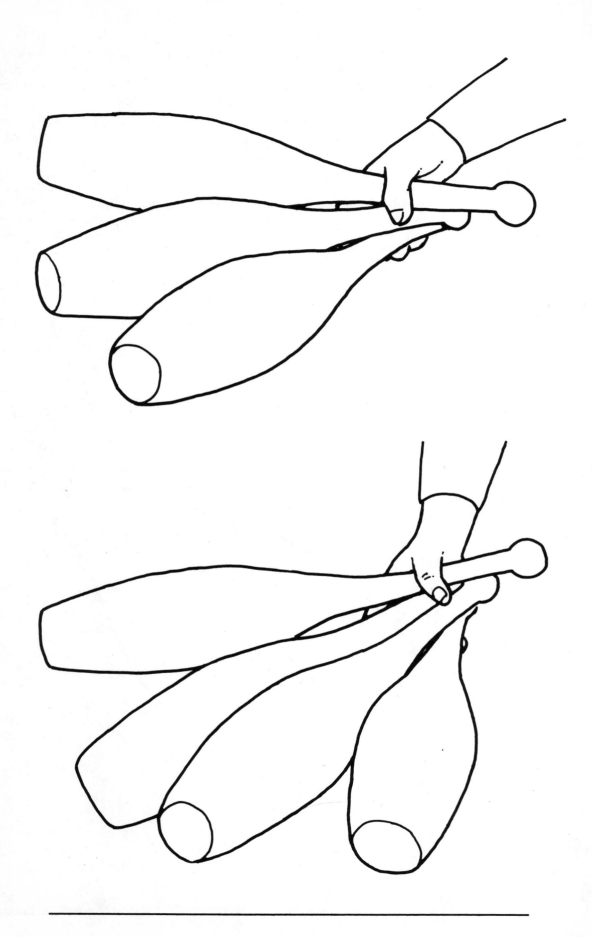

Start with the club that is on the bottom with your palm up. To start 3 or 4 clubs out of one hand, hold 2 clubs as just explained. The other clubs go underneath the first clubs with the body to the inside and the knobs to the outside. Always throw the clubs from the bottom of the stack first. With clubs you should throw and catch the clubs from the center of the handle.

3 clubs are most commonly juggled in single spins in a cascade pattern. For 4 or 5 clubs use double flips. For 6 or 7 clubs do triple flips.

For juggling 5, 6 or 7 clubs it is easier to use thinner, lighter clubs. For numbers, relative use of the forearm versus wrist in achieving flips on the clubs helps. For body throws, let the club slide to the knob as you are releasing it, while still keeping your thumb or index finger on part of the handle for control. Clubs with longer handles work better for body throws.

The author with a club I made to use for juggling 7 clubs.

3 CLUB STARTS   A common start for 3 clubs is to hold 2 clubs together with one hand and place the third club underneath and to the center of the other 2. The bottom club should extend forward about two to three inches. Throw the clubs so that the 2 on the top do double flips, and the single club on the bottom does a triple flip. It helps to concentrate on just the 2 clubs, but make sure that the single club goes straight up. This start can be done with the 3 clubs held with one hand or using both hands.

Some different starts that can be done using this method are:

3 behind the back with one hand;

3 up pirouette;

3 up pirouette, catch 2, pirouette going into a juggle as the last club comes down.

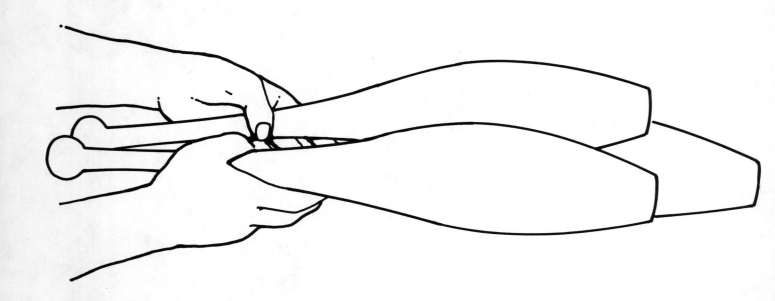

Backcrosses Singles   Every club is thrown behind your back, so that it goes around and behind your body with each hand solid in single spins. Make each throw about shoulder height. While juggling 3 clubs, first work on doing one throw behind your back. Remember that this trick is more of a lift over the shoulder of the opposite hand that is throwing the club. Next throw the same club back and forth behind your back. When learning 3 behind the back you may tend to throw too soon. It should be quite slow. Don't let your arm trail too far behind your back; you have to have time to get your hand back to catch the next club. Keep your back straight and turn your head from side to side as far as you can to see the throw coming.

Backcrosses Doubles   For double back crosses look straight up. Make every throw come over the opposite shoulder. You have to lift the club up with the whole arm as you release it behind your back. Try not to let your arm go behind your back very far. This is a slow trick; wait until the club reaches its peak before throwing the next throw.

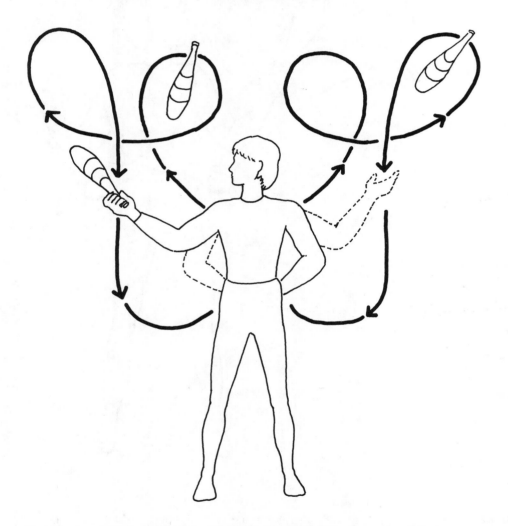

Backcrosses Triples   Since you are throwing triples, this is a very slow trick. Because of that you can concentrate on every throw. Try to keep as relaxed as possible. Look straight up above your head. This trick can be done with each club thrown individually, or throw a flash and throw the clubs back up again in a flash.

Under The Arm   The throw goes under the arm in a single spin. When you make the throw you have to be sure that it goes under your arm toward your elbow, and not under your wrist. The throw should be made parallel with the shoulders. Give the club some lift as it is released. Turn your head from side to side to see the incoming throw.

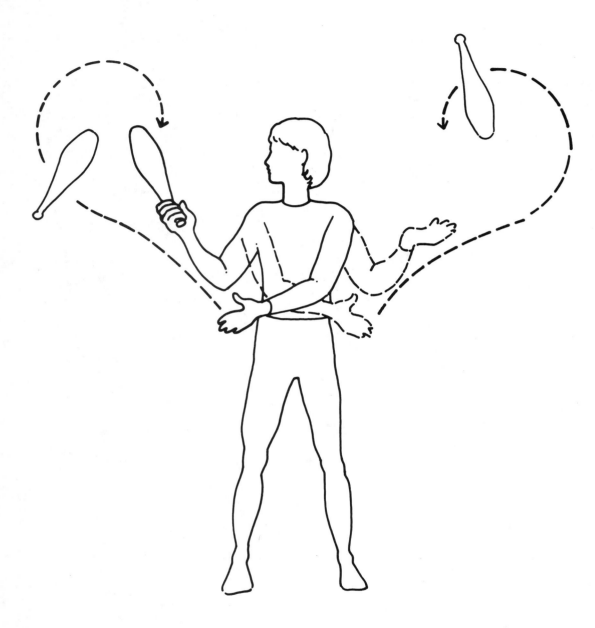

Arm, Arm, Back, Back   Throw an under the arm with each hand. Then throw two behind the back throws starting with the hand that you started the under the arm throw with. Keep your throws parallel with the shoulders. You have to keep your speed down as much as possible; it is not really all that fast a trick. You will have to move your hips forward and back as you throw 2 front and 2 back.

Single, Double Chops   As you are doing a cascade, swing the club down to the center of the pattern before you release the club under your wrist. A single chop would be chops done with single spins on the clubs as they are thrown; a double would be two spins. Make sure to swing the club quickly through the pattern. It looks best to swing the club in as large a circle as possible before it is released. When the club is released under your arm, it looks nice to let the club go very wide and bend the knees as you chop to each side.

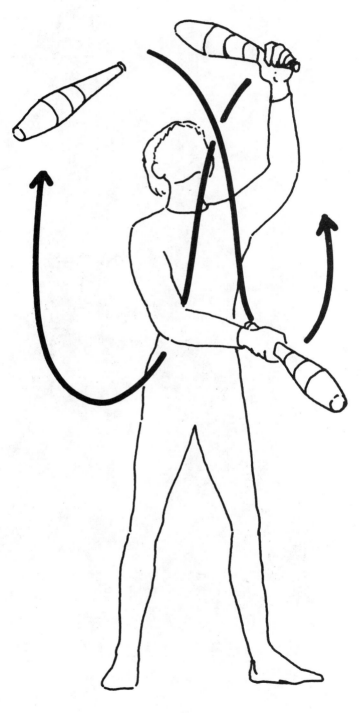

KIT SUMMERS-JUGGLING WITH FINESSE

Chops with Ken Benge.

Alberts   This is a throw from the front, toward the back, sent between your legs without lifting them; the club will go around one leg without lifting the leg. I named this trick after Albert Lucas, who was the first person that I saw doing the trick, even though others, such as Fudi, Ron Hennon, and Rudy Horn, did it earlier. This trick looks best when you stand up as straight as you can. When doing this you really have to slide to the knob of the club before it is thrown. Try to get your wrist through between your legs as far as possible. The knob on the club pivots in your fingers. Throw the club so that it comes over between your hip and your shoulder. This trick is really a lift of the club. Lift the club up and toward the front. You can do this using singles or doubles.

Trebla   (Albert spelled backwards.) The throw goes from the back to the front between the legs without lifting them. This trick also looks best when you are standing with your body as straight as you can. As you release the club, bend back slightly and get your wrist as far as you can between your legs. Once you have the club in position, lift it straight up into the pattern.

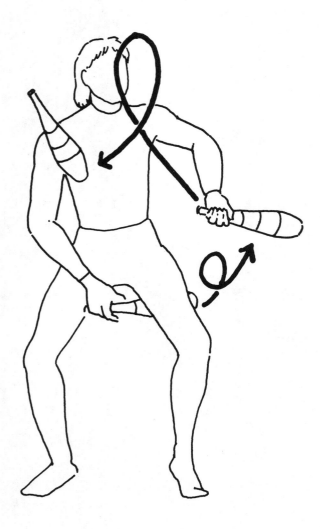

Albert throws.

Kit Summers,
watching Kit
throw trebla
throws.

Chop Chop, Back Back   This is done with single flips on the clubs. Do a chop with each hand, and immediately do a behind the back throw with each hand. After a chop is complete with one hand, the club is promptly thrown behind the back. This is done with each hand. If you are right handed you throw a right back throw, left back, immediately right chop, left chop, then go directly into this sequence again.

Chop Chop, Albert Albert   This is done with single spins. Do a chop with each hand, then immediately do an Albert throw with each hand. See chop chop, back back; but instead of doing two back throws, do two Albert throws.

Four Ways   This is one Albert with each hand, followed directly by one trebla with each hand. To start this, the first throw that you do is a trebla with one hand. Then start doing an Albert with each hand, then a trebla with each hand. Keep your body very straight for this trick. Your hands and the throws have to be kept low. Two Albert throws followed immediately by two trebla throws.

Six Ways   Each hand does a trebla, a back throw, than an Albert every throw. To explain this I will write R for right hand, L left, B back, T trebla, A Albert. So you do RT, LA, RB, LT, RA, LB. When you are learning this trick, it helps to have someone read these directions to you as you are practicing. Once again remain as upright as possible. Work on just throwing the body throws using one hand first, then only the other, finally combine the two.

Joggle   Each hand throws solid under each leg. You have to lift your leg as the club is released. Try not to lift your leg very much when making the throw. You have to extend your arm as much as you can when you make the throw, while lifting your leg only slightly. Another way in which to joggle, which was made famous by Bill Giduz, is to run as fast as you can while juggling 3 objects.

Joggle With 3 clubs, Rejean St. Jules.

Over Head   Juggle 3 clubs directly over your head. Bring 1 club out of a cascade directly over your head and start a cascade above your head. This is more of a lift than a throw; you have to push the club up. Angle the throws as you would do in a normal cascade in front of you.

Chins   As you catch the club, place the knob on your chin with the body up, then let it fall into your other hand. Juggle in a cascade with your hands held high. Bring a club up and place it on your chin. The club should balance momentarily before it falls into your other hand. Practice this doing a chin with only 1 club at first to get the feel of it.

Flat on Head   When you catch the club, place it on your head with the knob to the front. When you set the club on your head, set it so that it will stay there momentarily; then grab it off with the other hand when the space comes around.

Head Spin   Do the flat on head, but when you place the club on your head, spin it so that it spins one revolution before you catch it with your other hand. For this trick first work on using just one club and get the spin down before you try it while juggling. I have seen people get up to 4 spins while doing the head spin.

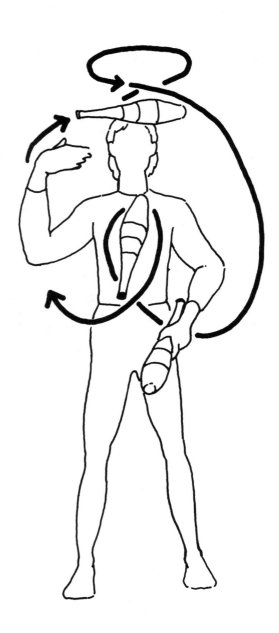

Head Snap

As you place the club on your chin (see Chins), let the club fall back and then snap your head forward to make the club do a single flip before you catch the club in your other hand. When you make the snap, balance the club momentarily and then bring your head forward quickly.

Head Roll

Do a head roll with a club. See head roll under 3 balls. With clubs, do the head roll with the knob out in front of your face. You will have to concentrate on keeping the club straight as you roll it. Try to roll it slowly.

Behind Back, Off Chin

Do an off the chin with every throw from one hand; while the other hand throws behind your back on every throw. Bring your behind the back throws forward more than usual to give you room to bring the club to your chin. Eye level for his trick should be kept high.

Throw, Catch Each Side Behind Back

Throw a double flip straight up on the same side as the hand that is throwing it. With the other hand, take the club that is in this hand behind your back and throw a double; then as the hand is still behind your back catch the double that was first thrown. Then do the same thing on the opposite side. This is a slow trick; do not try to do it too fast.

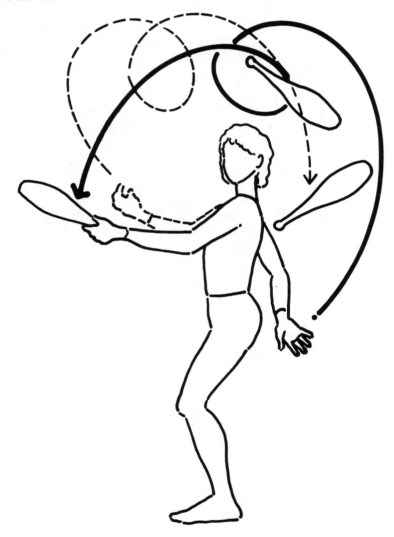

Reverse Hand Catch   Catch the club in your hand with your palm up and your hand turned so that the fingers are on the outside with the little finger forward. You can't have very much angle on the club when it is thrown to this hand. Turn your shoulder in as the club is caught. It helps to get your fingers as far forward as you can. Keep your elbow straight as the club is caught.

Flat Shower   Do a shower in double flips above your head, but throw the club so that it spins parallel with the shoulders, with the body on the outside as the club is released. Keep your hands and your eyesight high for the catches and throws. When the club is passed to the showering hand, have the knob down, and the body up.

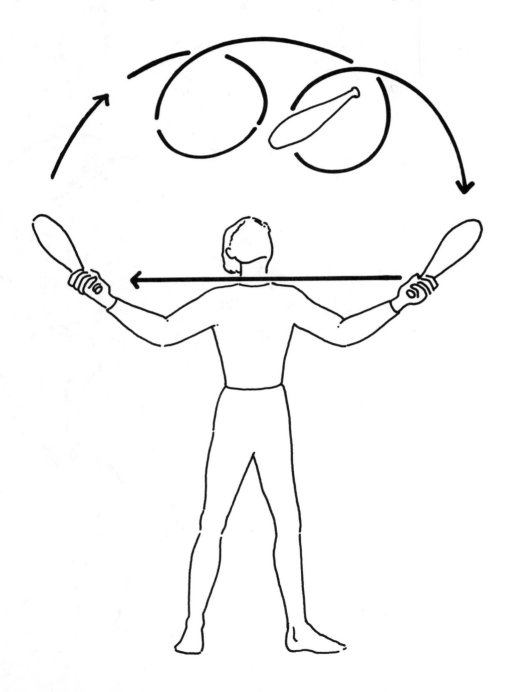

Slap Back   While doing a normal cascade, when the club comes around, instead of catching it, slap the handle so that it spins one rotation in the opposite direction and then is caught and thrown in a single spin back into the pattern. You will have to slap the club so hard that it will spin quickly enough to come around in time to throw it back into your cascade pattern. This trick can be done solid with each hand.

Throw to Balance on Foot   As you are doing a cascade, throw one club so that it makes one flip and then lands, knob first, on your foot in a balance. You do not put very much spin on the club since it is going to your foot. You might refer to the chapter on balancing to understand how to balance and what can be done with a balance on the foot.

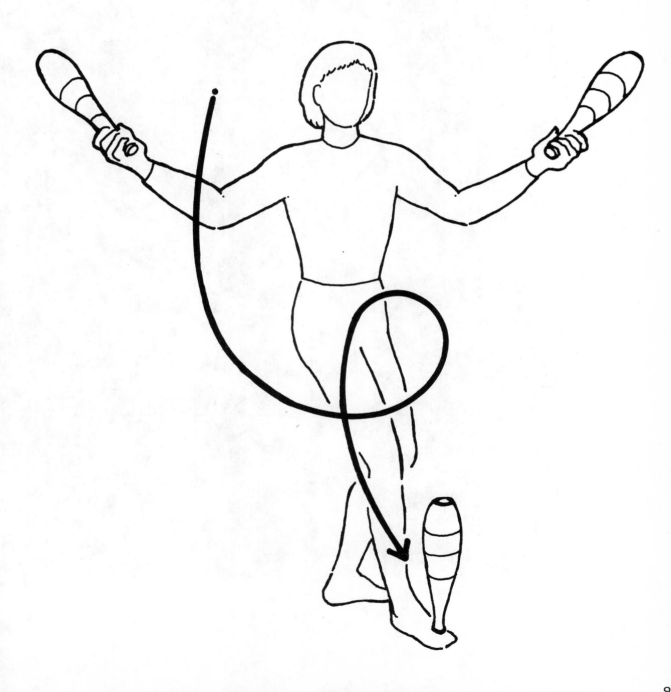

Kick Up   Lay the club across your foot with the body to the outside and toward the front. You will have to raise your toes and keep them raised the whole time that you are doing this. Then quickly bring the foot that has the club straight up and toward the outside. The club will do one spin before it is caught.

Kick up, Rejean St. Jules.

Cross Foot Kick Up   As you are juggling, place a club across your foot with the body to the inside. At the same time that you are doing this, step over the club with the other foot. Be sure to raise your toes as the club is placed on your foot. Then quickly bring the foot that has the club straight up and toward the outside. The club will do a single spin before it is caught.

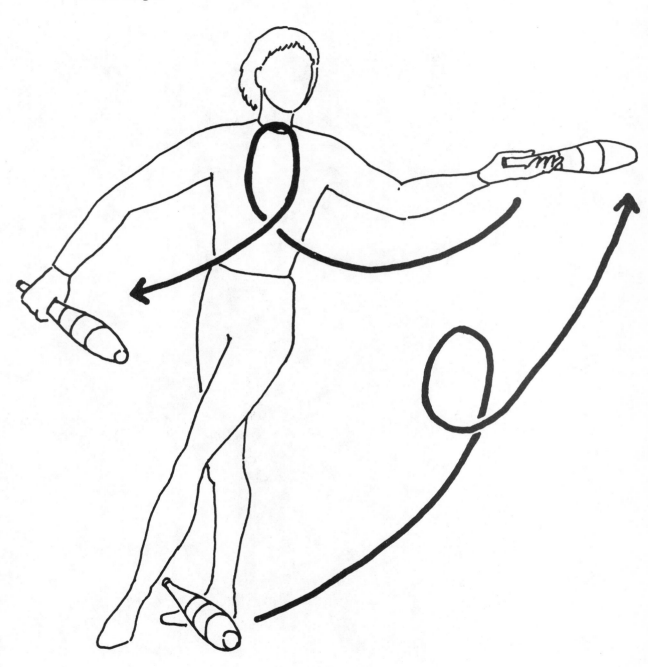

*The cross foot kick up, Kit
Summers.*

Slap Kick   As a club is lying on the ground with the handle away from you, quickly tap the end of the club with your foot so that it does a complete flip, or a half-flip to your hand and you go into a juggle. You will have to bend your knees as you reach down for the club. Your first two throws should be thrown in your normal cascade pattern as you reach down for the club.

Pirouettes   When you pirouette you have to pick a point in front of you to spot on. Try and always keep focused on that spot as you turn. Pirouettes can be done using floaters, or using one or more spins. When you pirouette using 1 club, it looks good to do something with the other clubs. You can trail the clubs behind you next to your body as you pirouette, or raise them straight up over your head. The easiest way to pirouette using 2 clubs thrown out of a cascade is to throw them both at the same time out of a 1 up, 2 up pattern. For 3 clubs do triple flips in columns throwing them right side first, then left side, then center. With columns you can throw the clubs right back up for another pirouette and do not have to pause. You have to do a quick flash with the clubs in triples. Make sure that the clubs are all released into the pattern completely before turning the pirouette.

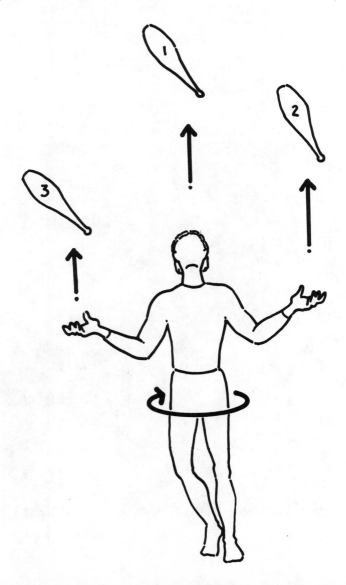

3 Club FINISHES

A basic finish for 3 clubs is to throw a double flip; then hand 1 club from the hand in which you want to catch the last club, and then catch this last club.

Behind the Back Finish

Throw a double flip straight up above one hand; then pass the club that is in the other hand to the hand that threw the double flip; bring your empty hand behind your back and catch the double that you first threw.

Last Club Caught Between the Other 2

Throw a double flip straight up. Transfer 1 club to the other hand with the knob underneath; catch the double between the 2 clubs by the handle as it is sliding toward the knob. This club is trapped between the other 2 clubs.

• 4 CLUBS •

The basic pattern for 4 clubs is 2 clubs in each hand doing double flips in outward circles, off sync. Begin by working on juggling 2 clubs in one hand in outward circles. The throws should be thrown so that they arc out toward the side, making a long oval. Then work on the other hand. When you are working on 2 clubs in one hand, try not to turn in a circle as you are doing it; keep facing the same direction. Now work on 4 clubs. Count your throws so that you can judge improvement. Once you have started to learn the 4 Clubs in off sync, work on 4 clubs on sync. Now work on going from off sync into sync and then back to off sync again.

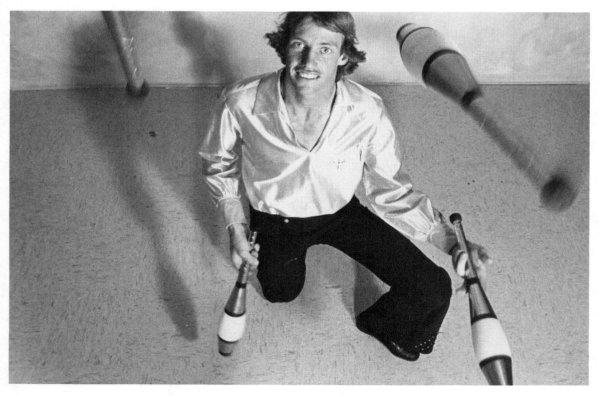

4 clubs on one knee, Kit Summers.

4 CLUB STARTS
Kick-Up

Place a club in the kick-up position (see 3 club kick up earlier in the book), either in normal kick up position, or cross foot kick up. Juggle 3 clubs and throw a double flip on the side of the body where the club will be coming after it is kicked up. As soon as the double is thrown you have to kick the club into the pattern. The other hand goes immediately into 2 in one hand in outward circles, double flips.

4 Up

Hold 2 clubs together so that they are parallel with each other. Then place 2 clubs below these clubs about three inches forward. Throw the 4 clubs straight up so that the top 2 clubs do double flips, and the bottom 2 clubs do triple flips.

4 Up Pirouette

Do the 4 up start. After you throw them do a pirouette before catching the clubs and going into an on sync juggle. Make sure that the 4 clubs are released and on their way up before starting the pirouette.

4 Up Pirouette, Pirouette

Go over the 4 up pirouette again. For this trick throw the clubs so that the 2 lower clubs do quads, and the 2 higher clubs do triples. After the clubs are thrown, pirouette, catch 2 clubs, then pirouette once again holding the 2 clubs that you caught first. When the other 2 clubs come down, go into an on sync juggle.

4 CLUB TRICKS
Flat Front

Start throwing off sync from the outside to the inside. As you are doing this, bring the pattern parallel with the shoulders so that all of the throws are thrown so they look flat to someone looking at it from the front. Keep the pattern close to the body.

Ready for the prom, doing the flat front,
Kit Summers.

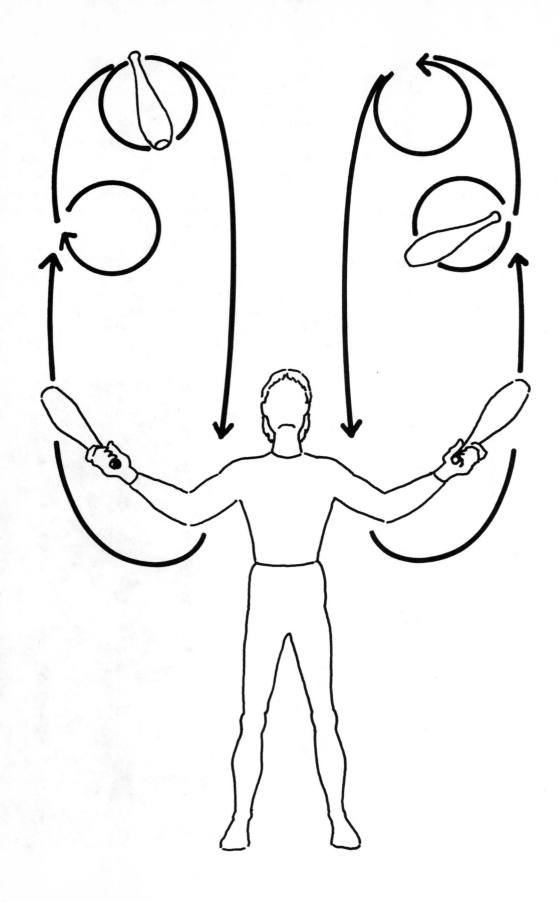

Triple, Single   Throw triple flips with one hand and throw single flips with the other hand. Try to relax the single spin that you are throwing; concentrate on the triple spins. This trick can be done throwing the triple flip over the shoulder, under the leg, behind the back, or over the top of the pattern in flat throws.

1 High   As your are juggling 4 clubs off-sync, throw one club up in a quad throw to the same side as the hand that is throwing it, then do 2 single spins with the other 3 clubs in a cascade pattern. Go into 4 club double spins fountain pattern when the quad comes down again.

1 High Continues   Do the one high and as the club is coming down, after one single throw in a cascade with the hand that you threw the quad with, throw another quad. Your other hand will throw 1 single, then a double. So one hand throws a quad, then a single to the other hand. Your other hand throws a double, then a single to the other hand. Your attention should be focused on juggling the 3 clubs up until the quad is about to land in your hand. It helps me to think about releasing the quad sooner than I need.

Flat Half Shower   Do a half shower with triples and singles and throw the triples over the top of the pattern from the outside. The throws that are going over the top should be thrown flat.

Flat Shower   Do a shower with the clubs, but make your throws parallel with the shoulders as the club is thrown. For this trick keep the throws that are passed about face level. Turn the catching hand palm out before you catch the club.

Pairs with Flat Shower   As you are doing a flat shower, instead of throwing a club, save it and place a second club underneath with the body to the inside, about three inches beyond the club that is already there. Throw the 2 clubs so that the bottom club that is extended does a quad and the other club does a triple. Catch them separately as they come down and hand them across to the showering hand as you would do normally.

Shoulders   As you are juggling off sync, throw a club over the same shoulder as the hand that is throwing it. You will have to slide toward the knob of the club before you release it. Try to angle the throw so that the body of the club is away from you. Bring your hand straight up as the club is released. This can be done solid with each hand. The primary concern is keeping each side separate.

Spread   Juggle on sync. As you are doing this, throw 2 clubs on one side of the other 2 and keep the pattern going throwing columns. Do not try to go too fast when doing this. Wait until the last moment to throw the next pair. You should try to relax as much as possible when doing this. Move your hips and shoulders to each side when making the catch.

Round the World Spread

While doing a spread, throw 2 clubs on one side underneath the other 2, and then throw each pair of clubs under the other 2 while traveling in a circle. As the clubs are released, the handles should be angled back toward you. The way I thought of this trick was I wanted to run off stage after doing the spread by throwing the pairs of clubs under the other pair as I ran. I would have had to run too fast to keep up with the clubs, so I turned in a circle.

Chop Chop, to Spread

As you are doing 4 clubs off sync, save one club and catch a second club underneath this club. Do a chop with the 2 clubs in one hand (see chops under 3 clubs) to the center of the other 2 clubs. Do a second chop with the hand that has one club on the other side and send it up with the other single club. Release the 2 together as doubles, so that they split a little. Go into a spread after you do the second chop with the other hand.

Single, Double Over the Shoulder

See "Shoulders" just explained. For this trick throw a single with one hand, and a double over your shoulder with the other hand. Turn your shoulder in and make the shoulder throws go to a center point. Concentrate more on the throws going over your shoulder to your other hand.

Barrett Felker, throwing a single spin from the left hand, and a double spin over the shoulder with his right hand.

2 Behind Back, Same Time

Juggle on sync, throw both clubs behind your back by crossing your hands behind your back before you release the clubs. One club has to cross in front of the other club. Try to make them both travel the same height and the same placement. Keep in mind that this trick is more of a lift.

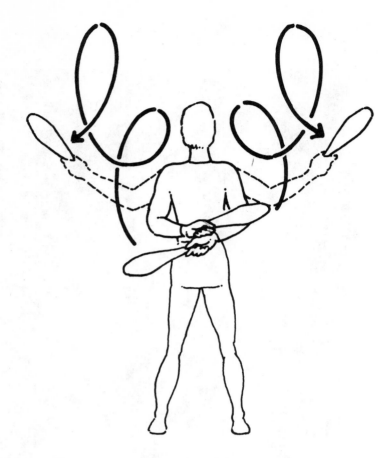

2, 4 Up Pirouette, Half Pirouette

While doing 4 club doubles in on sync, throw 2 clubs up in triples and do a pirouette while holding the other 2 clubs. Or throw all 4 clubs up and do a pirouette. A half pirouette can also be done using this method. Make sure that the clubs are released completely before you turn the pirouette.

4 CLUB FINISHES

I once read that the first person to incorporate a 4 club juggle in his act had to complete the juggle by having the curtain lowered because he didn't know how to stop. The following is one suggestion on a finish that you can use. Throw a triple flip out of one hand, catch the other 2 clubs in your other hand as you're putting the third club under your arm. Then catch the triple flip in your empty hand.

• 5 CLUBS •

The peak points of your pattern should be wide and higher for this pattern. Work on just throwing doubles with 3 clubs for a while. Now work on doing a flash with 3 clubs and immediately throw the clubs back up in a flash. Now have 3 clubs in your starting hand and throw them to the other hand and catch the 3 clubs. Work on throwing the 3 clubs to the other hand and then immediately throw the clubs back to the first hand. This would be doing 3 clubs in a 5 club pattern with two empty spaces. Try to make the 3 throws as quickly as you would when doing 5 clubs. Now work on flashing the 5 clubs. It will be hard work at first to catch the flash. And now work on juggling 5 clubs; a steady rhythm is very important. Be sure to angle your throws enough into the pattern. Count your throws to judge progress.

The author juggling 5 clubs (with a drum roll).

5 CLUB STARTS
First Club Quad

Hold all 5 clubs. Throw 1 club in a quad, when it comes down go into a cascade putting the other club into the pattern after it is caught. Make sure you start throwing the other 4 clubs soon enough.

Forehead Balance to 5

Balance 1 club on your forehead and have 2 clubs in each hand. Let the club that is being balanced fall forward. As it is falling forward, throw the other 4 clubs into a cascade pattern with double flips and go into a cascade putting the other club into the pattern after it is caught. You will have to practice the release of the 4 clubs for a while to learn the correct timing to go into a cascade.

Kick Up

This is explained for the club being kicked up to the right hand. With the club in kick up position, juggle 4 clubs in a fountain pattern and then cross the throw from the right hand to the left hand. Then cross 2 throws from the left hand and at the same time kick the club up to the right hand and go into a cascade, so you cross right, then 2 left hand throws and kick, then go into a cascade.

5 clubs a piece, Dan Holzman and Barry Friedman.

5 CLUB TRICKS
Doubles Behind Back, One Side

Backcrosses

As you are doing a cascade, start to throw behind the back with one hand in double flips. Be sure to bring your throws from behind the back far enough forward so that you do not turn. You have to remain with your shoulders going the same direction the entire time that you are doing this trick.

As you are doing a cascade pattern with 5 clubs, start throwing each throw behind your back solid with each hand in triple flips. To learn this, first use 3 clubs, work on throwing triple back crosses solid very slowly. Try to get each throw very precise. Now work on flashing 3 clubs up quickly behind your back in triples; then send them right back up again in triples behind your back. When you do backcrosses with 5 clubs you throw 3 behind your back, then pause slightly, then throw the fourth club. Pause momentarily once again, and finally throw the fifth club and go into backcrosses. You have to pause to get the timing change going from doubles to triples. Do not let your hand travel very far behind your back as you release the club, you have to get your hand to the front again for the next club.

Peter Davison, being cool while throwing 5 club backcrosses.

JACK BREMLOV

1 High   Throw a quad on one side of the pattern out of a cascade. After throwing the quad catch the other 4 clubs, two in hand, the second club on each side underneath the first. As the quad is coming down, throw the 4 back into a cascade in the correct timing to catch the quad and put it into the pattern. You have to tense up to throw the quad, then relax after you catch the other 4.

5 High Columns   As you are doing a cascade in doubles, throw a triple on one side of the pattern, a triple on the outside on the other side, triple up to the inside next to the first club. The fourth club thrown goes next to the second club thrown, and the fifth club a triple in the middle of the other 4 clubs. This is a flash from doubles to triples. Go back into a cascade with doubles as the clubs come back down. When learning this trick keep your columns narrow, but as you improve on the trick, make your columns wider. It looks better to the audience when you keep your pattern wide.

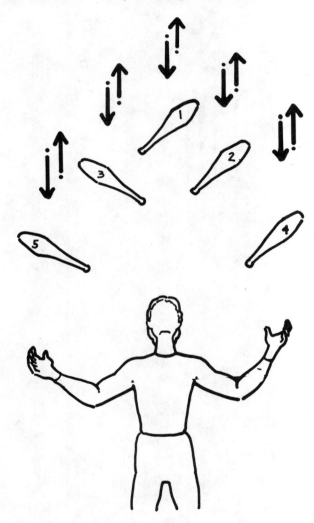

3, 5 Up Pirouette   Do a cascade in doubles: throw either 3 clubs up in triples and hold the other 2 clubs while you turn, or throw all 5 clubs up in triples. Turn a pirouette. Always make sure that the clubs are all released before turning. You really have to concentrate on keeping the triples from colliding as they are going up.

Juggle 6 clubs with 3 in each hand doing triple flips, outward circles, off sync timing. Work on juggling 3 clubs in each hand alone for awhile. Try not to turn while you are doing this. With 6 clubs you have to concentrate hard on keeping each side separate from the other. Fudi, from Hungary, did 6 clubs while he was here juggling with Ringling Brothers and Barnum and Bailey Circus. I met him in Sweden when he was performing in a circus there. He performs with his wife Suzi. They do a fast paced act with passing and also solo juggling.

Using 6 clubs, Anthony Gatto.

For 7 clubs it helps to use very lightweight, narrow clubs. I found that juggling 7 clubs was easier than juggling 6 clubs because there was less chance of collision. 7 clubs are juggled in triple flips in a cascade pattern. Accuracy of throws is the key to juggling 7 clubs. It is important to get the first 5 clubs released quickly. Keep your pattern as wide as possible. Keep the handles angled in toward you.

At this time Sorin Munteanus performs mostly in Europe. He does a fantastic act in which he includes the juggling of 7 clubs. I met him when I was on a trip to Europe. I practiced with him for a few hours one day. He had such control with the 7, I was very impressed. One of the first people in the world to juggle 7 clubs was Jack Bremlov from Czechoslovakia. We have never met, but we have been writing to each other for many years. He does not speak English, and I do not speak Czech, so we each have to get the letters translated when we receive them.

JACK BREMLOV

WITH 7

FIRST IN THE WORLD

Anthony Gatto, 7 clubs.

• 22 CLUBS •

Hold 2 clubs with each finger. The thumb holds one club more. Throw them thumb club first. Do a cascade in triple flips. This pattern should be juggled while standing on one leg, with each throw going under your left ear lobe. If you do learn this trick please write to Guinness immediately!

• SUMMARY: JUGGLING WITH CLUBS •

— Keep the clubs low and precise.

— Keep your elbows up and out.

— Keep the pattern wider than with balls.

— Point the tip of the club to a point above your other hand.

— Keep your wrists strong when throwing the clubs.

— Keep the hand relaxed until the club hits it.

— Keep your basic cascade pattern down below your face.

— You might want to wear a helmet (more comedy).

SEVEN
BALANCING

Most people have a natural sense of balance: a feeling for the center of gravity of an object. People use balancing in everyday living to steady a glass of water, to ride a bike, and to walk.

Balancing is used in juggling quite often and this chapter will help you to improve your balancing. There have been many famous balancers. Rudy Horn included a trick in his act in which he would lay a teaspoon on his foot and then kick it up to a balance on his forehead.

Enrico Rastelli, balancing with multi balls.

Because it has a higher center of gravity, it is easier to balance a longer object that is heavier on the top, for example a pool cue balanced with the thinner, lighter end down. When you are first learning to balance, use the center of your palm to balance. Keep your hand as flat as possible. Keep your eyes on the top portion of the object being balanced.

To learn to balance well, use a broom stick until you can balance it. Once you have mastered balancing the broomstick, cut off six inches and then master this length. Cut off an additional six inches until you reach the length that you want to be able to balance.

Balancing a spoon, Pepito Alvarez.

Do not over-compensate when making a save on an object being balanced. Rather than concentrating too much on saving an object that is falling, concentrate on correcting the problem before it happens. Try to stay very relaxed while balancing.

When you have to, it is best to move the bottom of the object being balanced from side to side rather than forward and backward. Try not to let the top move; instead maneuver the bottom under the top. If the object is falling, it helps to lower it in one quick movement, thus giving it less gravitational pull.

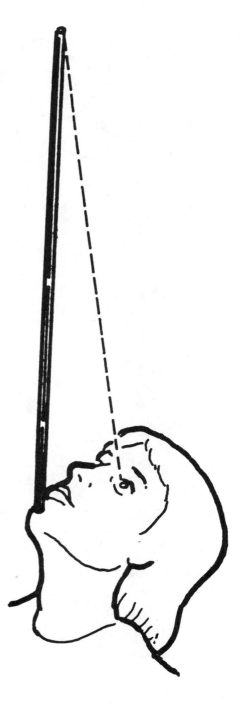

Balancing while looking at the top of the object.

Experiment with balancing different objects. An object such as a pencil, spoon, or straight stick is a one-dimensional balance.

Also, try balancing two-dimensional objects, such as a juggling ring or a plate. Three-dimensional objects can be balanced by picking a point on the object that would be the main center of weight of the object being balanced. Examples of three-dimensional objects would be a hat, a chair, or a piano. Different objects can also be stacked together and balanced as one.

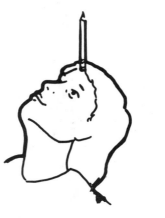 

(drawing by Peter Davison)

Learn to balance with your hand, chin, nose, forehead, foot, knee, elbow, shoulder, ear, or wherever else you can think of. You just have to be able to see the top of the object being balanced. Balancing with the limbs is easiest though, because you will be able to move more quickly to make a save on an object that is falling. You can also balance things on other objects, such as using a stick as an extention of your hand. A peacock feather is very easy to balance. Use the air resistance to assist you.

EDWARD JACKMAN

Juggling while balancing a bike on his face, Edward Jackman.

When juggling clubs, tennis rackets, or a similar item, you can balance them by placing them wherever you want to balance them while you are juggling them. You can also throw the object to a balance while juggling it. You can juggle most anything while you are doing a balance. It looks very impressive to an audience to see someone juggle while doing a balance.

When you balance something on your face, use your forehead to balance with, so that the audience can see the rest of your face.

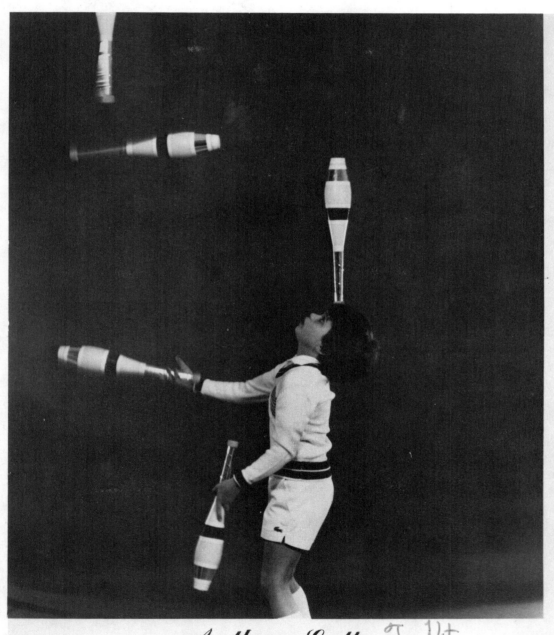

Anthony Gatto To Kit,
your friend Anthony

When you get good at balancing something on your chin or forehead, try kneeling down with the object being balanced. Then lie down; touch the back of your head almost to the floor; then stand once again, still maintaining the balance.

To balance a pool cue on your chin, and one on each thumb, your cone of vision must include all of the objects being balanced. This trick is a lot more difficult than it looks to the audience.

Ron Meyers, balancing 3 pool cues.

Enrico Rastelli, balancing with multi balls.

Igor Rudenko, balancing various places.

One trick that looks very impressive and dangerous to an audience is to use a knife for a mouthstick and balance a sword on it point to point. To set this up, flatten the point of the knife slightly, and then use a small dentist drill to drill a hole in the end of the knife that you have flattened a bit. Balance with point of the sword in this hole. Before trying this trick, make sure that you are an accomplished balancer and are very sure of yourself.

Using a knife as a mouth stick and juggling 4 rings,
Ken Benge.

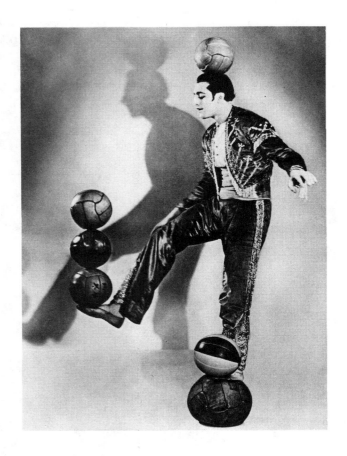

Balancing, Maximilian Truzzi.

Jon Held started juggling at the same time that I began. We practiced together every day for years. For a while we did an act together in San Diego. He went on to juggle with the fantastic jugglers Peter Davison and Kazia Tennembaum. The next routine is one that Jon did: Some balancing feats (feets?) that can be done with a balance on your foot are the following (these are done with the knob of the club down): Throw a club, one flip, to a balance on the foot, or drop it straight down to the foot from the hand. Pass the club from the foot where it is balancing on to the other foot. Drop the club to kick-up position and kick the club up to a balance on your foot. Lift the club from your foot to a balance on your chin. Finally, let the club fall from your chin into your hand and go into a juggle.

• SUMMARY: BALANCING •

— Look at the top of the object being balanced.
— Stay relaxed.
— Do not move quickly.

— If you must move, try to move from side to side when making a save.
— Have confidence!

EIGHT
JUGGLING VARIOUS ITEMS

There are more objects to juggle with than balls, rings, and clubs. This chapter deals with examples of some of the great variety of things that can be juggled. Really anything can be juggled, balanced, or manipulated in some way. I have gotten into the habit of trying to think of some way that something could be used as a juggling object for everything I see. These are sample ideas for you to use. Exercise your imagination to think of other ways and things that can be used.

JOYCE RICE   "Dazzler In Motion"

Years ago there were jugglers known as gentlemen jugglers, or salon jugglers. On stage there would be a room setting from a house. The juggler would come in and use everything in the room to juggle with. Felix Adanos was one of the greatest gentlemen jugglers. He manipulated everything from pool cues, to picture frames, to candle sticks. I have never actually met Adanos, but we have been corresponding for years. He is a very friendly man and gave me many ideas. A person that is bringing back gentlemen juggling is Daniel Holzman. Daniel was recently staying over with me, and at seven in the morning he was out practicing. He does some great moves.

ADANOS

Tommy Curtin, competing at the 1981 International Juggling Convention, amazed his audience. They were used to seeing only balls, clubs, and rings. Tommy also juggled with these objects, but in an innovative and very different way, along with juggling various items. Tommy is a good friend of mine and I admire his juggling very much. This shows you how impressive the juggling of various items can be. By the way, Tommy won the competition!

Juggling various items, Felix Adanos.

CLAY BALL TRICK

Juggle a ball of clay and two balls that have a good bounce. As you are juggling, bounce one lacrosse ball, then juggle again. Bounce the other ball, continuing to juggle when it bounces up. Last, throw the ball of clay and act as if you expect it to bounce up to your hand. It will plop on the ground and stay there. Your audience will expect the ball to bounce up like the other balls did. Boy, will they be surprised! Make sure that the clay ball is the same size as the other balls you are juggling.

CROQUET BALLS

Juggle one soft ball and two croquet balls. Throw the soft ball straight up. When it comes down, let it bounce off your head. Smack the crochet balls together as it hits your head. It seems as if the wooden ball put a dent in your head.

BEACH BALLS

Juggle beach balls in columns using both hands. This is a slow trick. The beach balls seem to float in the air. Start practicing with two balls, but three are not hard to juggle in this manner.

BALLS WITH LIGHT INSIDE

Get plastic shells made that hold a light inside that can be turned on. Use these lit balls to juggle in the dark. It looks good to make each ball a different color. The great juggler Rudy Horn did this trick in his act.

MAGIC AND JUGGLING

Incorporate magic into your juggling and impress an even larger audience. Here are a few suggestions. All of these tricks are available at your local magic shop:

The silk cylinder: Juggle the silks, then put them into the cylinder. When you make the balls appear, juggle with the balls.

Linking rings: Do a routine with the three single rings. Then juggle the three rings. When you end the juggle, quickly put the three rings behind your back, then continue the routine after you get the rings that weren't used for the juggling.

Multiplying billiard balls: After you do your routine, juggle with three balls.

Cups and balls: Finish the routine by producing three juggling balls, then juggle them.

FLOURESCENT PROPS

Paint your props with fluorescent paint. Use these to juggle under a blacklight, perhaps wearing a costume also painted with fluorescent paint. The props will leave a trail as they are traveling.

BURNING NEWSPAPER

Make a cone out of a sheet of newspaper. With the point down, light the top of the cone. Balance the burning cone, point down, on your nose while juggling. Balance the cone while it is on fire as long as you can on your nose, then quickly pull your face away. While doing this trick, be careful of falling pieces of burning newspaper.

HAMMER AND NAILS

Use a board that has some nails started into it. Juggle 3 hammers and as each one lands in your hand, hit a nail so that they all get pounded into the board. The act is livelier if you use music in the background and then pound to the music.

PING PONG BALLS

Juggle ping pong balls using your mouth and shoot them into the air using your diaphragm. I've heard of 1, 2, 3, 4, 5, 6, and 7 being done in this manner, using air and the muscles of the diaphragm to shoot the ball into the air. To catch the ball you have to extend your tongue and have the ping pong ball land on it. Then you quickly take the ball into your mouth and shoot it out again. For three and five, try to do a cascade pattern. For five and seven you can also use your hands to feed them into your mouth. Place them into your mouth after you have caught them with your hand.

There have been a few very good ping pong ball jugglers (or as I like to call them, pongs). One of the first people to do the pongs with his mouth was Gran Picasso. It is said that he thought of doing this trick because he became bored when he worked in his father's vineyard, and used to do grapes in this manner. I met Picasso in 1977 while he was performing in Las Vegas. He does a very fast act which includes the pongs, frisbees, and a fast three ball routine.

GRAN PICASO

Tony Ferco does an act with his family, two men and two women. He has included five pongs in his act without a hand-feed. He doesn't just do a flash; he holds it for a short while. I once heard that he performed seven pongs without a hand-feed. If you ever get the chance to meet Tony and his family you will see that they are wonderful people.

Dick Franco not only does pongs with his mouth, he adds pirouettes and dance moves. He has been performing pongs for many years, and is very good with them.

DICK FRANCO

MOON JUGGLING Fly to the moon and juggle. With the lower gravity you should be able to do 89½ balls. Of course you may want to practice holding your breath so you needn't be encumbered by a bulky space suit. I heard word that the man on the moon is a closet juggler.

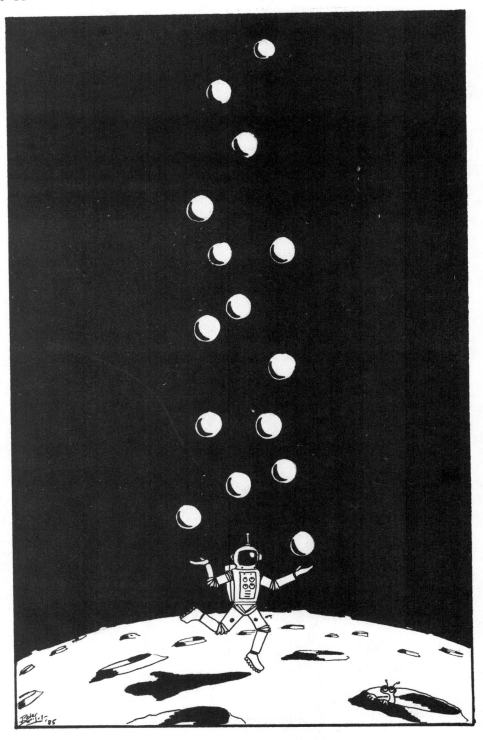

(drawing by Peter Davison)

BICYCLE HOOPS   Use old wooden bicycle rims, or fiberglass hoops, for juggling. They can be rolled up your back, down your back, across your shoulders, or on the ground. Also 5 hoops can be rolled on the ground in a cascade pattern by angling the top of the hoops toward you as they are rolled out behind you. Hoop rolling was popular around the turn of the century. At that time there were many famous hoop-rollers. Nowadays there are only a few people around the world doing it. One of the best hoop-rollers ever is Bob Bramson. I met Bob in Germany. He does an act with his wife Liz. He rolls 3 hoops down and also up his back, using each hand; he does a routine rolling 5 hoops on the floor; he juggles 7 smaller hoops in the air. Bob and Liz also do a few rolling routines together. I spent a couple of days with the Bramson's and saw many of their shows. In each show, I was amazed by his level of skill.

Carter Brown did not want to juggle the usual balls, clubs, and rings. He took up hoop rolling instead. We have been friends for years, and I have seen Carter advance to become a very good hoop juggler.

When I began juggling again after the accident, I had to start at the beginning once again. But I didn't get the thrill that you can get when learning a new trick, because I had already had that thrill once. I took up hoop rolling because it was totally different, and I could get the thrill again because it was not something that I had done before the accident. I had a lot of fun learning hoop rolling.

Bob Bramson, rolling hoops down his back in a shower pattern.

Handling 3 hoops, Carter Brown.

The author rolling 5 hoops in a cascade pattern.

UMBRELLAS   Umbrellas can be juggled open or closed. You may have to modify the umbrella so that it can be juggled. In order to counteract the open umbrella turning too slowly, you may want to add some weight to the handle. It looks very good to add a spring which will open the umbrellas instantly by pressing a lever at the bottom of the handle. Juggle with the umbrellas in the closed position, push the button thus releasing the umbrellas, and then juggle with the umbrellas in the open position. It is actually easier to juggle with the umbrellas in the open position, although it looks harder to the audience. Eva Vida includes the trick in her wonderful act. She ends it by stacking the open umbrellas one on top of the other two, and then hides behind them.

Juggling 3 umbrellas, Eva Vida.

BALL ON UMBRELLA

To spin a ball on an open umbrella, first get the umbrella turning with the top up and the handle down, at about shoulder level. Then place the ball in the center of one side of the umbrella as it is spinning. Adjust the speed of the umbrella to keep the ball in place. To do this trick you have to have the ball rolling up a slight incline, so angle the umbrella as you are rolling the ball.

GAG BALL ON UMBRELLA

Spin a ball on an umbrella. When you finish, close up the umbrella, and put it over your shoulder. Let the audience see that the ball is attached to the umbrella on a string.

WATER ON UMBRELLA

Have an umbrella and a bottle of liquid that has a mouth on the bottle that can fit over the end of the umbrella. Open the umbrella; throw the bottle so that it lands, mouth first, on the metal end of the top of the umbrella. Stand under the umbrella and catch the bottle on the end of the umbrella by the mouth of the bottle. The umbrella will protect you from the liquid coming down.

Another routine for this is to put a cork in the bottle so that the liquid will not spill out when the bottle is juggled, but can be pushed inside the bottle. The umbrella should have a switch at the end of the handle that can be pressed to instantly open the umbrella. Juggle with the bottle, umbrella, and a rain hat. To finish, place the hat on your head. Throw the bottle so that it will land cork end first, on the metal end of the umbrella. After the bottle is caught, quickly release the umbrella so that you will be protected from the water.

FRISBEES You can juggle frisbees by angling your throws up and out so that they come back to you by catching the air as they go up. Shower your throws so that they go up on top of the pattern, and return below these throws. An impressive variation is to angle your throws out over the heads of the audience and have them return to you. Mexican sombreros and boomerangs can also be juggled in this manner.

4 frisbees, Yehya Awada.

Using hats as frisbees, Tommy Curtin.

CUPS AND SAUCERS   For this trick use cups and saucers that fit together very easily. For the first plate you have to use plaster of paris on the bottom to make a mold of your head to make the plate fit easily on your head. Lay this first saucer top down on your foot. Kick the saucer so that it turns a half flip going up to land on your head. Now place a cup over your toes. Kick the cup so that it also turns a half flip and lands in the saucer. Keep doing this until you have a stack of cups and saucers. As you release the cups and saucers from your foot, try and bring you foot up as high as possible. It is more of a lift than a kick. Do not lower your head much to catch the cups and saucers. Keep your head on the same plane. A good finish for this trick is to kick a sugar cube into the top cup, then a teaspoon. This is a trick that the great juggler Rudy Horn included in his act, while on a tall unicycle!

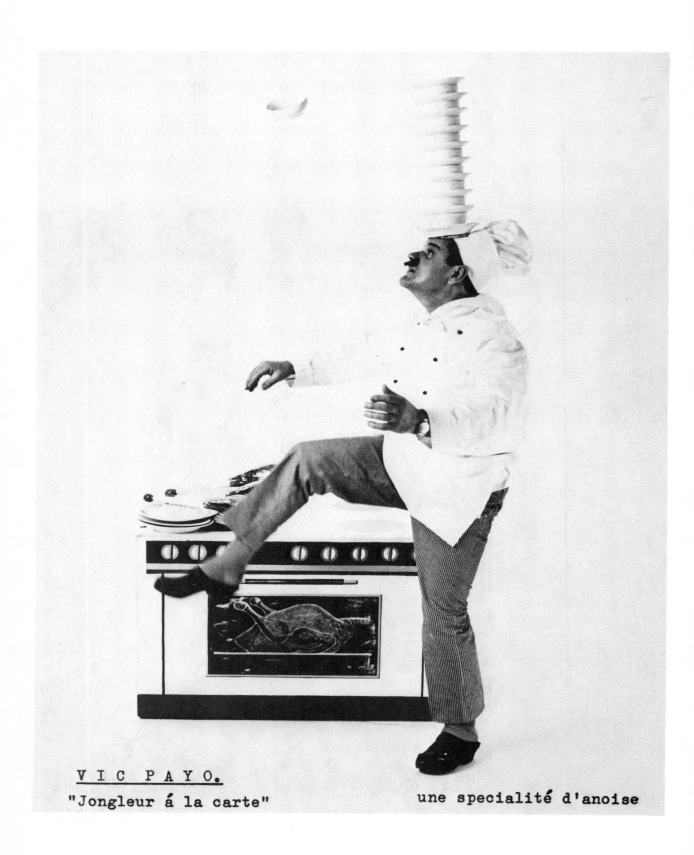

VIC PAYO.
"Jongleur á la carte"   une specialité d'anoise

144

Rudy Horn doing the finish of Cups and Saucers.

BANJOS   Use banjos to juggle. Have each banjo tuned to a different note. As the banjo comes around and is caught, pluck the strings and play a tune. This is from a write up on Franco Piper: "...Mr. Piper snatches up a third instrument and sends it to join its fellows aloft. Everybody is on the tip-toe of expectation for a big smash-which does not come, however. In regular rhythm, the trio of banjos rise and fall to their own music. Another snatch from the table, and lo! There are four banjos flying through space, sending forth a wild, but unwavering volume of sounds.

Below, as cool as the proverbial cucumber, stands Mr. Piper, his arms hands, and fingers working like so many wheels in a machine throwing, catching, and playing with all the nonchalance of the professional juggler. And this is maintained for some minutes without the slightest sign of worry. When the tune is finished, the four banjos are nimbly caught by their mainipulator, two in each hand, and restored to their former resting place."

HAT, VIOLIN, BOW   With a hat on your head, use a violin and bow to play a song. Then throw the bow into the air, grab the hat off your head with your empty hand. Then juggle the hat, violin, and bow. Finish by placing the hat back onto your head, and finish playing your song.

Hat, violin, and bow juggling, Kip Konwiser.

PUPPIES   Juggle using live puppies. You have to be careful when doing this to avoid getting bitten by the angry puppies. This really isn't very nice to the little guys, and your audience might get angry with you and leave.

DANIEL ROSEN

Daniel Rosen, poor little puppies!

FOOT JUGGLING   Use an angled table that has supports that go against your shoulders to keep you from sliding while you are lying on your back on the table. You can use your feet to manipulate different objects. Some of the best in the world at foot juggling are The Castors. One of the brothers, Toly, also does a wonderful comedy juggling act by juggling balls, boxes, and hats. I met them in Europe, and I was amazed at what they could do with their feet.

Lee James, juggling 6 balls with his hands and feet.

Foot juggling, the Castors.

DRUM   Use a drum to bounce balls off, throwing from the outside. It is better to build your own drum using wood that has a good bounce for the balls that you are using. Learn to bounce balls off the floor before using the drum. You can either bounce the balls straight down, or have the drum about five feet in front of you angled toward you. Rudy Horn was famous for this trick, using 7 balls to bounce off the drum!

DRUM STICKS OR DRUM MALLETS   Stand over a drum and juggle 3 drum sticks or mallets. As you are juggling them bring the head of the stick or mallet down and strike the drum. You can do this solid with each hand. To change the beat, throw doubles or triples.

Multi balls on multi drums, Lulu Perezoff.

Playing the drum, Lothar Lohr.

Force bouncing 7 balls off a drum, Rudy Horn.

TENNIS RACKET   Use a tennis racket in one hand as you juggle 3 balls. Hold the racket in one hand and use the strings to bounce the balls.

Using a tennis racket as one hand, Dale Jones.

SELF DEFENSE   Juggling is good for self defense. When you are practicing and someone wants to attack you, just do some chops and you will look so tough that they will run away scared. If this doesn't work, then break out the machetes and torches and start juggling them.

SATURN TRICK   Juggle with 2 rings in one hand, and 2 balls in the other, in an on sync pattern. Start throwing the balls through the rings. You have to be very accurate with the throws of the balls.

ALAN HOWARD

SPOONS INTO GLASSES   Have a board with a row of glasses attached. Lay spoons on the board with the handles going toward the glasses. Hold the board with both hands and flip the spoons up so that they do a half flip and land in the glasses, all at the same time.

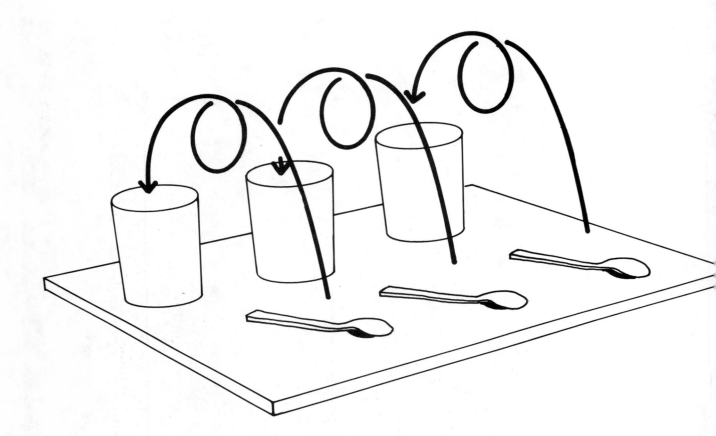

HEADSTAND   Make a stand that will support you while you are standing on your head. It should be cup shaped to fit the top of your head. With your free arms you can juggle props by pushing them up, or bounce balls off the floor or a drum.

This is a trick that Bobby May originated. Known as "The International Juggler," Bobby May was born February 20, 1907. He became one the of the best and most famous jugglers of our time. May started juggling at the age of 12 after seeing a tramp juggler, Phil Latoska, at the Grant Theater in Cleveland, Ohio, Bobby's home town. May played amateur nights until he got his first professional engagement in 1922 at Luna Park in Cleveland. He did a team act from 1925 to 1927 known as Joe Cody and

Brother. In their act, Joe did the comedy while Bobby did the straight juggling. In the fall of 1928, Bobby started doing a single act with some dancing and patter with club, ball and hat juggling. In 1942, he began the skating portion of his life by putting his act on ice. He was first with "The Skating Vanities." He went on to skate with Sonja Henie in "Ice Revue," and "Holiday on Ice." Most of his travels after 1958 took him outside the country. One review of his act from 1950 said, "What this boy May does with the whirling clubs and a handful of small rubber balls is amazing. This guy is not only stupendous, he's colossal. Why, he stands on his head on a platform five feet off the ice and does an upside down juggling stunt, bouncing 5 balls off a drum."

   I remember the first time I met Bobby. Jon Held and I were on our way to the International Jugglers Convention in Delaware; we went up to the door, both scared, and rang the doorbell. Neither of us knew what to expect. When Bobby answered the door, we told him that we were jugglers and just wanted to meet him. He gave us a smile and said, "Come on in. How long do you want to stay? We have a room upstairs for you to stay in." We were both relieved and at that point we knew what a wonderful person he was.

Bobby May, standing on his head while bouncing 3 balls off a drum.

PLATE SPINNING   Use ¼ inch wooden dowels that are approximately 4 feet long, and attach the wooden dowels to a board. Use plates or bowls that have a ring on the bottom. Place the plate on the dowel and start it spinning. With your other hand grasp the dowel at its center and move it so that it gets the plate turning. This trick is easily built up. Get a couple of plates spinning, and then try to do something else, like juggling 8 rings (see 8 ring juggle). Get back to the plates before they fall. Now get all the plates spinning, juggle the 8 rings, then grab off all of the plates before they fall. Before I saw Erich Breen, I had not seen very many good plate spinning acts. Watching him fascinated me. He is one of the best in the world. I met him when I was in Europe seeing the jugglers who were performing over there. He not only does outstanding plate spinning, but his juggling is very good also.

Plate spinning, Erich Brenn.

APPLE EATING   Juggle with an apple and 2 other props. As the apple is caught with one hand, bring it quickly to your mouth and take a bite out of the apple. You have to bring the apple to your mouth very quickly when doing this trick. For a comedy ending, juggle the 2 objects in one hand and use your other hand to eat the apple. Make sure that the apple doesn't have a worm in it before you do the trick. This trick has been used by jugglers for centuries. It is a big part of Mark Neisser's act.

APPLE, FORK, NAPKIN   As you are juggling these props, do the apple eating as just explained. Use the napkin to wipe your mouth as you are juggling it. To finish, throw the apple into the air and place the fork in your mouth. When the apple comes down, catch it on the fork above your head, then wipe your chin with the napkin.

FRUITS AND VEGETABLES   Any fruits and vegetables can be juggled, and you do not have to be a vegetarian to do it. See apple eating to see what you can do with edible fruits and vegetables. A comedy line for juggling vegetables is "This is going to be a real good tossed salad." Try juggling a banana, and peel it as you are juggling it. My mom has never been safe in the grocery store with me around.

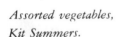

Assorted vegetables,
Kit Summers.

ICE CUBES   Juggle ice cubes until they melt. This can be very boring for your audience though. You might try doing a tap dance routine while you are doing it, or do it while you are in the Sahara Desert.

EGGS   This is an easy trick to build; it is also easy to get good comedy using eggs. When you juggle eggs, remember that when you finish the juggling of the 3 eggs, do not catch an egg on top of another egg; they'll break (I did this the first time I juggled eggs).

HAT, GLOVES AND CANE   Come on stage with a hat and gloves on and using a straight cane. Do a routine balancing the cane. Then take off the gloves, and roll them into a ball. Juggle with the ball of gloves, the cane, and the hat. You might want to do this routine to the tune of "Putting on the Ritz."

BILLIARD BALL RACK   Build a rack as in the drawing. The rack is balanced on your forehead. Then start throwing balls up into it, and as they drop out, shower them back up into the rack again. Don't go too fast while doing this.

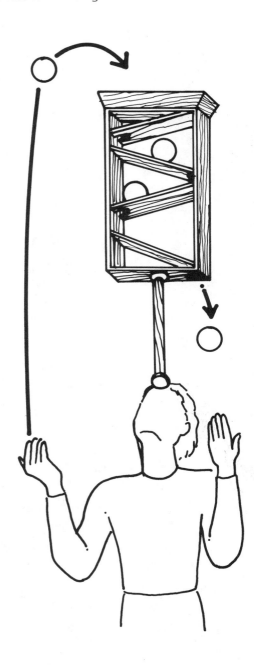

SCARVES

To juggle scarves, use an over-hand grab down on the scarf. Juggling scarves is very slow. It looks good to turn in a circle while showering 3 scarves. See how far apart you can juggle 4 while doing a spread.

COLOR CHANGING RINGS

Use rings that are colored one color on one side and a different color on the other side. As you are juggling the rings with one side of them toward the audience, grab the rings so that you turn them over and have the other side of the ring facing the audience. The audience will see a different color as you turn the rings over.

POOL TABLE POCKETS

Use a belt with pockets that are about the size of pool table pockets. They should have a metal ring to keep the top open. Place the pockets on the belt at each hip, and one directly in the center of the back. As you juggle balls, throw one ball high, when it comes down, catch it in a pocket. This can be developed into an entire act by itself.

John McPeak, pool table pockets.

JACK BREMLOV

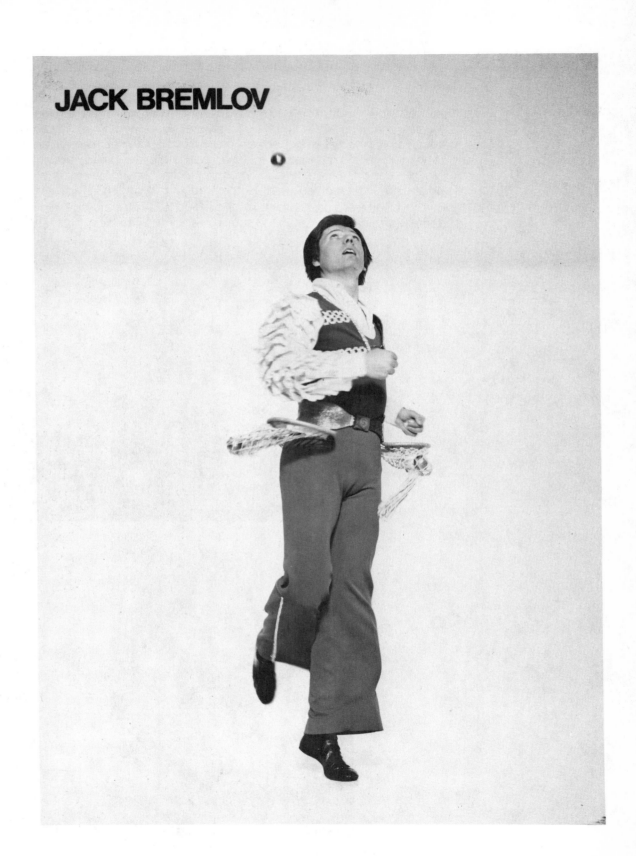

MACHETES AND KNIVES

Be sure that your are very adept at juggling clubs before you try to conquer machetes or knives. After purchasing some machetes or knives, use a ginder, or a file, to dull the blades. Don't be stupid and juggle with sharp machetes, there is no need or reason to do so. You should be able to juggle the machetes by the blades, rather than the handles. You may also have to modify the handle for juggling. The main thing about juggling machetes is that you have to get over your fear of them. Once you get over your fear, the machetes are just like clubs. First start with one machete and two clubs. When you can do this well try two machetes and a club. Finally do the 3 machetes. Machetes and knives have been used in juggling acts for years. They are a major portion of Jeff Chromen's act. He performs mostly around California. He is very inventive and tells stories as he is juggling. He said, "I mostly just use the machetes for comedy. It is easy to create good comedy using the machetes."

The author juggling 3 machetes.

Randy Foster, 3 deadly sickles.

MARK NIZER

TORCHES Before trying torches, you should have complete control over 3 clubs. Torches are best juggled outdoors, for safety sake. It is scary, but not all that dangerous to catch the wrong end, and quickly throw the torch to the other hand to be caught by the handle. After you dip your torches in the fuel, shake off the excess fuel and replace the cap on the fuel can before lighting them. Hold the torches up and away from you, and anyone else, before you light them. Some of the tricks that look very good with torches are backcrosses, chops, and torch swinging (this is club swinging with 2 torches).

MARK NIZER

Kit Summers, 3 torches in the park.

3 torch juggling, Rejean St. Jules.

3 torch juggling, Ernst Montego

CHAINSAWS   Buy the smallest chainsaws that you can find. Bolt a wooden handle on to each chainsaw. Remove the cutting teeth from the chain on the saws. Then juggle the chainsaws. The smoke and the noise are very impressive to an audience. It might help to practice juggling heavy objects before trying the chainsaws. You might also have the saw blades running and be able to push a hidden button to turn them off before juggling them.

Dick Franco juggling 3 chainsaws.

HEAD PEDESTAL   Use a pedestal that will fit on your head and hold 1 ball. You can juggle anything while you have this balanced on your forehead.

LOTTIE BRUNN

Using a head pedestal, Lottie Brunn.

MOUTHSTICK   Use a stick about one inch in diameter that is fitted with a piece that can be held in your mouth. As you are holding it solidly between your teeth, you can spin a ball on the tip of it (see ball spinning), balance a ball at about the center of the stick, or catch a ball that is thrown from the audience.

Using a mouthstick, Michael Chirrick.

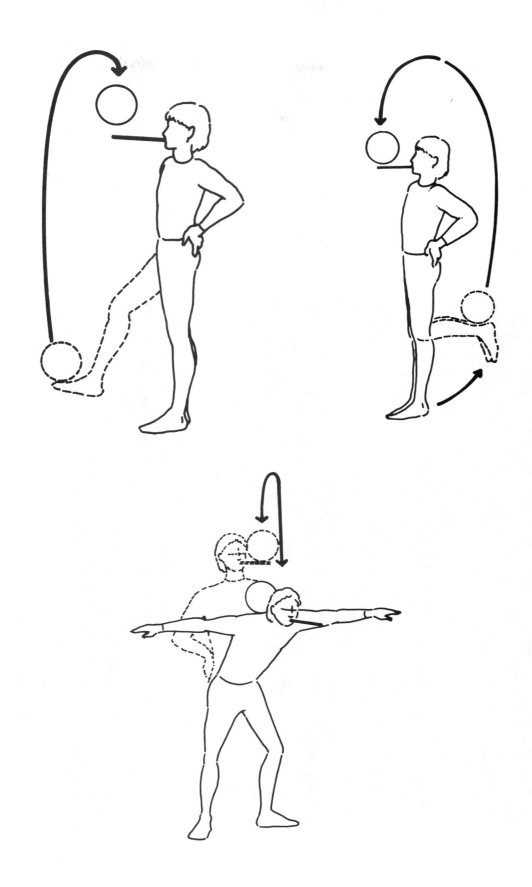

ARM SPIN   Spin 3 rings on your arm. Spin one near your wrist, one ring right below your elbow, and the last ring between your shoulder and elbow. The rings should be spun in opposite directions.

LEG SPIN   You can spin 2 rings on your leg. Spin 1 ring on your ankle, and 1 ring in the middle of your upper leg between your knee and hip. The rings should spin in opposite directions. You have to sort of kick your foot forward in time to keep the rings spinning.

MOUTHSTICK SPIN   Rings can be spun on a mouthstick. Use your neck to keep the ring spinning.

Swinging on arms and leg, Liz Bramson.

• BALL SPINNING AND MANIPULATION •

Ball spinning is related to juggling in that the two can be mixed by spinning while juggling. To see a person spin a ball on one finger can amaze most any audience. Two of the best ball spinners are Francis and Lottie Brunn. What they can do with a spinning ball is amazing.

Lottie's son, Michael Chirrick, is also a wonderful ballspinner. He combines a lot of dance with his juggling. He does a very clean act in which he juggles torches, balls, and he also does some amazing ball spinning. I have known Mike for some time and if you get the chance to see him you will be amazed at his ball spinning. Ball spinning seems to be an up and coming trend where I live in San Diego. It seems like everyone around here is learning to spin a ball. One of the better up and coming ball spinners is Mark Neisser. Mark is learning new tricks all of the time. Another new ball spinner in the San Diego area is Tash Wesp. She does a trick in which she wears a mask that has a long nose. She spins a ball and places it on the tip of the mask nose while she is looking up. It's really very funny looking.

Spinning a ball, Lana Reed.

MARK NIZER

For ball spinning, use balls that have a good grip and are inflated almost all the way. To spin a ball, grip the ball from below and spin it so that it spins counterclockwise with the left hand, and clockwise with the right hand. Spin the ball so that it is spinning horizontally up to your finger. Learn to spin a ball with either hand so that you can do tricks using a spinning ball with each hand at the same time. The faster you can spin the ball, the longer it will spin. If you spin the ball on the tip of your fingernail, it will spin longer. Try to give the ball a quick snap when sending it up to your index finger. As you do tricks with ball spinning, have the ball move in a vertical, straight up and down motion as much as possible. A few tricks that can be done with 1 ball spinning are the following:

With a ball spinning on your finger, rotate your arm taking the ball to the inside of your arm. Bring it all the way around your elbow to the front again. The ball should go in a straight up and down motion as much as possible. This trick can also be done taking the ball in the opposite direction.

Take the ball down and under your arm. Continue taking the ball behind your back, then transfer the ball while still spinning it to the other hand. Take the ball back to the front again.

As the ball is spinning, lift the ball straight up so that it is thrown into the air then catch it again, still spinning, on the same finger, or the index finger of the other hand. When you catch the ball you will have to go down in time with the ball a little; it is a catch. The ball can also be thrown under your leg, behind your back, or you can do a pirouette with the ball in the air.

With the ball spinning, you can use the other hand to juggle.

Do a cartwheel with a ball spinning by using the hand that is not spinning the ball to support yourself. You take the ball to the inside and under your arm. Try to keep the ball on the same horizontal plane when doing the cartwheel.

• 2 BALL SPINNING •

Spin 1 ball on the index finger of each hand.

Spin 1 ball and place another ball in the center on the top of the spinning ball. Start the second ball rotating in the same direction as the first ball. The spinning ball will keep the other ball in place. You will have to move the ball that is spinning on the bottom under the center point of the ball that is placed on top.

Place a ball on the point of a mouthstick. Anything can be juggled while you have the ball spinning on a mouthstick.

Have a ball between your heels. Spin a ball on each hand. Lift the ball that is between your heels with your feet so that it goes over your head. When it comes down, bounce the ball on your head with 2 balls spinning.

Spin a ball on 1 finger. Kick a second ball from between your heels straight over your head so that it lands on top of the ball spinning. This can also be done with a ball spinning on each hand.

With 2 balls spinning, take one ball down and under your arm. As you are bringing it back up, do the same thing with the other hand. When you are doing this continually you will be doing a swimming motion with your arms.

Michael Chirrick, doing a forward roll while spinning 3 balls.

Spin one ball on the index finger of your choice; spin 2 rings on this same arm; have a ball on a mouthstick; have a ball on a head pedestal; spin 2 rings on one leg; juggle 3 rings in the hand that is not spinning the ball; and yes, do all of these things at the same time! To begin, have 2 rings on your arm at your shoulder. Start the rings spinning on your leg, one near the ankle and the other directly above your knee. Place the mouthstick in your mouth and put a ball on it; put the head pedestal on your head; spin a ball on the index finger of one hand; start the 2 rings spinning on the same arm between your shoulder and your elbow in opposite directions. Finally juggle the 3 rings in one hand. Work on each part of the Brunn finish individually before trying them all together.

The Brunn Finish,
Francis Brunn (originator).

This is a trick that Francis Brunn originated and made famous. His sister Lottie also performs the Brunn Finish. After all, she is a Brunn. Born Franzl Brunn in Germany, Francis Brunn started his professional career with his famous sister. They performed in Germany for a while. Then in 1948, they were brought to America by John Ringling North. When Francis first came to America he included the juggling of 10 rings in his act. After they were here for a while, Lottie put her own great act together and performed all over the world with it. Francis and Lottie both performed and worked with some of the most famous people on earth. As a solo act Francis Brunn performed on the same bill with Frank Sinatra, Danny Kaye, Judy Garland, Marlene Dietrich, The Beatles, George Burns, Jack Benny, Sammy Davis Jr., Jerry Lewis, Elvis Presley, and Bob Hope, to name a few. After I had my accident, I received a phone call from Francis, wondering how I was doing. That meant a great deal to me. Lottie is also a good friend of mine, and we correspond often.

Another member of the Brunn Family is Montego. He also does the Brunn finish, but he does something different. He performs it while on a unicycle!

Doing the Brunn Finish while on a unicycle, Ernst Montego.

LOTTIE BRUNN

Club swinging is very good for loosening up before a practice session. For many years it was used in gymnastics classes. Although it is seldom seen these days. Club swinging is not used just to develop the chest to the best advantage, but for the strengthening of the muscles of the arms, heart, and all the vital organs. Club swinging was recommended as an exercise in the past because of its attractiveness and overall toning.

Club swinging was done at the turn of the century with wooden Indian clubs, which were also the first clubs used for juggling. These clubs were heavy and club swinging was used as an exercise. The juggling of clubs naturally evolved from club swinging. During rest periods, the club swinger would play around with 1 or 2 clubs for diversion. It was only natural that eventually some pretty clever moves developed from those play periods and the juggling of clubs was born.

The author holding a swinging club
from 1912, 6¼ pounds!

Club swinging was reintroduced by Michael Moshen and Allan Jocobs. Allan went on to win the US Nationals competition at the 1983 International Juggling Convention in New York. He did a wonderful routine of club swinging and the juggling of 3 clubs. Seeing Allan's routine inspired jugglers to take up club swinging, and at the next convention, many people were proficient. If you ever get the chance to meet Allan you will see what a great person and good friend he can be, as I did.

Allan Jacobs swinging 2 torches.

Practice your club swinging in front of a mirror to work on form to make sure that your angles are correct, and that you are extending far enough with the hands. Performing club swinging looks great! It should be treated almost like a dance. Find music that will fit your routine well. Torch swinging looks very impressive too; the 2 torches leave a trail as they are swinging.

When swinging the club, hold it with a loose grip so that it can rotate easily in your hand. Swing it with just enough effort to keep it going, then merely direct it. When swinging, try to let the club do most of the work; let the swinging club bring the arm with it, rather than making the arm do all the work. After the club has started swinging, its own weight will almost do the work.

There are two grips that are used in club swinging. In the first of these, the ring grip, your thumb and forefinger encircle the knob of the prop you are using. In the second grip, the ball and socket grip, the knob is held deeply in the palm with your fingers and thumb all wrapped around the knob and extending down the handle of the club. The club rolls around loosely in a circle, the knob free to rotate completely. Keep your club swinging in two planes, parallel with the shoulders, and perpendicular to the shoulders.These will be called shoulder plane, and vertical body plane. Do circles in the shoulder plane using your wrists, elbows, and shoulders. Try to make your circles as accurate as possible. The three basic arm positions for the shoulder plane are with your arms at ninety degrees, straight to the side, and straight down. Different circles that you can do in the shoulder plane are shoulder circles, upper fronts, lower fronts, lower backs, and under arm circles. A large circle is one in which the shoulder is the center. A small circle is one in which the hand is the center. Learn all movements in one direction, and also in the opposite direction.

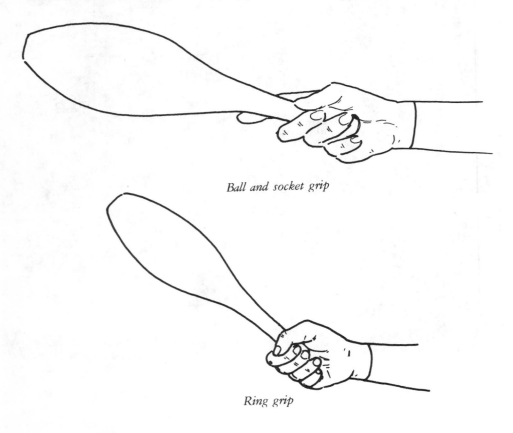

Ball and socket grip

Ring grip

Direction of Circles

Outer circles — Either one or both clubs pass sideways from the median line in front of the body.

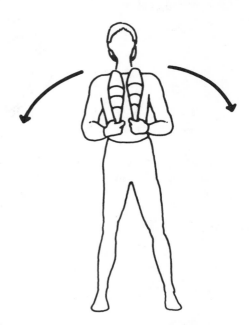

Inner-circles — Either one or both clubs pass toward the median line in front of the body.

Circles to the right — Both clubs pass to the right. The right club does an outer circle, and the left club does an inner circle.

Circles to the left — Both clubs pass to the left.

Forward Circles — One or both clubs pass forward.

Backward Circles — One or both clubs pass backward toward your face.

Outside Circles — Made by circling the clubs perpendicularly outside the arms, either forward or backward.

Inside Circles — Made by circling the clubs perpendicularly between the arms, either forward or backward.

Horizontal Circles — With the club extended horizontally, circle them on a horizontal plane to the right or left above or below the arms.

Snakes — Grasp the club by the knob and handle with the forefinger over the end of the knob. Have the club parallel with and against the forearm. Raise your elbow to a height equal to your shoulder. Flex the wrist and let the body of the club rest on your forearm, palm facing up and forward.

The snake consists of two circles, each circle going to the side away from the face. First circle, start the club circling away from the face, then to the side, and continue doing a small circle until the club passes underneath the forearm, palm facing down. At this point turn your hand so that it is now facing up. The second circle is done in front of the arm with the body of the club raised up above the elbow. Continue this until your hand circles around and when the arm is parallel once again, bring the club around to the starting point again.

When doing the snake, your elbow should be a stationary center point with the club traveling around this point. For doing reverse snakes, follow these same directions in the opposite order. I'm sorry to say that the snake should not be done in conjunction with torch swinging.

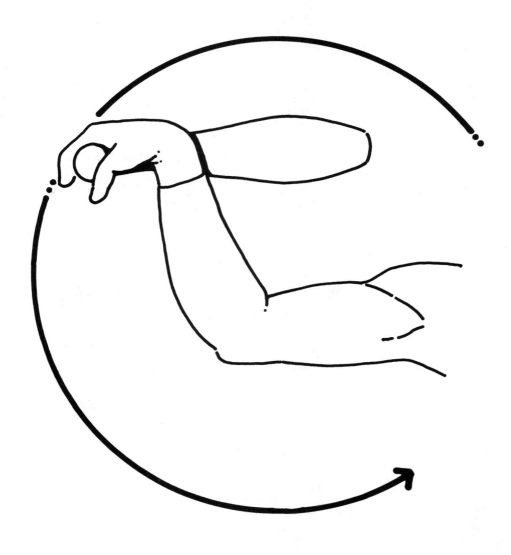

Different times for club swinging are the following. Learn all movements in one direction, and also in the opposite direction.

Parallel time: swinging one club in one direction, the other club does exactly the same move.

Follow time: one club does a circle and the other club does the same move, but one beat behind the first club.

Alternating time: a combination of two different movements with each hand.

Figure 8: Use the ring grip for this move. The direction of your swinging is in the vertical body plane with your swinging going away from your face. Each hand separately does two swings, on the far side of the body, and one swing on the near side of the body. To begin, drop one club down to your side and have the other club follow. In the first, swing both of the clubs, only do one swing on the first side; then go into two swings on the opposite side and one on the near side. This move should look like you are using one straight stick, with your wrists hooked together.

• HATS •

There have been many great hat jugglers. One of the best is Kris Kremo. He uses silk top hats that are reinforced. Rudy Schweitzer is also very good with hats. I met Rudy in Germany. He juggles with 3 balls, 3 boxes, and 3 hats. He is a very kind man, you will like him a lot if you ever get the chance to meet him.

In all of the tricks that I am mentioning, the hat is to be held by the brim with your fingers inside the hat. I am just listing some of the tricks that can be done with a single hat.

Tossing a hat onto head (drawing by Peter Davison).

Throw the hat one, two, or three flips and catch it on your head.

With your arm straight out in front of you, use you other hand and knock the hat so that it rolls down your arm; then catch it with the arm that it is rolling down. After it is caught, roll it back up to land on your head.

With the hat on your head, roll it straight down your back and catch it with one hand. Then roll it straight up your back and catch it once again on your head.

Throw the hat one flip and catch it on your foot. Then kick it up one flip to land back on your head. Also try to catch the hat by the brim in a balance on your nose.

Knock the hat off your head with one hand; let it drop to your knee and then land on your foot so that your toes go inside the hat. Then kick the hat one flip to land on your head again.

Come on stage wearing a hat. With your head you give a forward toss and the hat balances on your nose. The hat can be allowed to settle back on your head and again flipped to the balanced position. For a comedy climax you tilt your head still further forward to expose the fact that something beside skill is holding the hat in place. The something is simply a dark thread. One end you sew to one side of the hat; then take it behind your neck, and hook it to your collar. You'll have to experiment with the proper length of thread as well as the flipping of the hat up from your head.

Throw the hat one spin and catch it on your foot. Kick the hat from your foot over your head; do a half pirouette, and catch the hat on the same foot.

Balance a cane on your forehead; throw the hat in a single flip and have it land on the top of the cane with the opening down, still keeping the cane balanced. Then let the cane slide down your forehead to be caught in your hand. Let the hat land on your head.

To juggle 3 hats, throw them and catch them by the brim, with your fingers inside the hat. Throw the hats in a single flip to the other hand while doing a cascade pattern.

When the hat comes around one of the times, instead of catching it in your hand, catch the hat on your head. Take it off again by grabbing it by the front, thumb on the top of the brim, fingers pointing down. Then put the hat back into the juggle. The following are a few ideas that you can work on:

Throw a hat to a catch on your head. Flip another hat to your head. While this hat is in the air, use the same hand that you threw the hat with and take the hat off your head, and put it back into the juggle. You can also do this rolling the hats down your back instead of grabbing them off your head and throwing the hats in the air.

Drop 1 hat to a catch on your foot, then kick it in a single flip to a juggle again.

Shower the 3 hats by grabbing the hats off your head and throwing a single flip to the other hand, this hand placing the hat back on the head. You can also throw the hats behind your back, under the leg, or in an Albert throw.

Kris Kremo, 3 hats on the roof.

JACK BREMLOV

To Kit Summers
with all my best
wishes

Kris Kremo

Lido - Show - Stardust
Las Vegas Jan. 29. 1984

3 hat juggling, Kris Kremo.

• CIGAR BOXES •

W.C. Fields was famous for juggling cigar boxes. Born in Philadelphia, January 29, 1880, William Claude Dunkinfield, alias W.C. Fields, worked his way from poverty, past performing twenty times a day at Fortescue's Pier in Atlantic City, to top billing in vaudeville and motion pictures. His professional juggling career began at the age of 14 after seeing the vaudeville team of Burns Brothers. In tramp attire (because it made him feel natural and look older than he was), he developed a comedy juggling act that took him around the world.

Kris Kremo really puts a lot of character into juggling with cigar boxes. Bela Kremo, Kris's father, taught him juggling when Kris was very young. Kris made his first public performance at the age of twelve. For a while the two of them did a very exciting duo act. Kris is the only juggler to ever master doing a triple (yes triple!) pirouette with 3 boxes in the air. Kris has also completed a quadruple pirouette, which has never before been done. I met with Kris a number of times. After I had the accident, he sent me a very inspiring letter, which really helped me.

Charley Brown is an up and coming juggler. He does a good act in which he includes a 4 and 5 box routine. Charley recently visited me and he is working on new tricks all the time.

I did an act with cigar boxes for a few years. I liked cigar boxes because it was a good break from toss juggling. At the time of the accident I was working on doing a double pirouette with 3 boxes in the air.

• 3 BOXES •

When doing 3 cigar boxes, think of the 2 side boxes as an extension of your hands. Concentrate on manipulating the box that is in the center. When you are doing cigar boxes, move your body in an up and down motion as you are doing a move. Bring the boxes up to about chest high, then at the peak of the upward motion, complete the move as the boxes going down again.

With 3 boxes, Kit Summers.

Francisca BERARDY

Place the 3 boxes on edge, end to end, on the floor. The body bends over and the right hand grasps the right box, the left hand grasps the left box. Then stand straight with the boxes. The center box is held in position by the squeezing action of the other two boxes. With the boxes at waist high you are now ready to start doing cigar boxes.

PASS BOXES   Hand one of the end boxes to the other hand and then place it on the opposite end. This can also be done handing the box under your leg, behind your back, or behind your head.

GRAB CENTER BOX   Grab the center box and place the box on the end where your hand was at first. Rather than concentrate too much on grabbing the center box, think more about the box that will be the center box after you bring the center box around and catch the other 2 boxes.

Grabbing the center box, Gino.

GRAB END BOX

Grab the opposite end box and bring it to the starting position. You will have to bring the box out a little to the opposite side directly after you grab it, then bring the box under the other boxes and place it on the end.

GRAB END BOX, SWING AROUND OTHER 2

Grab the end box with the opposite hand, bring it all the way around the other 2 and place it back where you began when you grabbed the end box. You have to be very fast with this one. When you complete this trick your hands will be crossed. Your hands will fall into position on each end simultaneously.

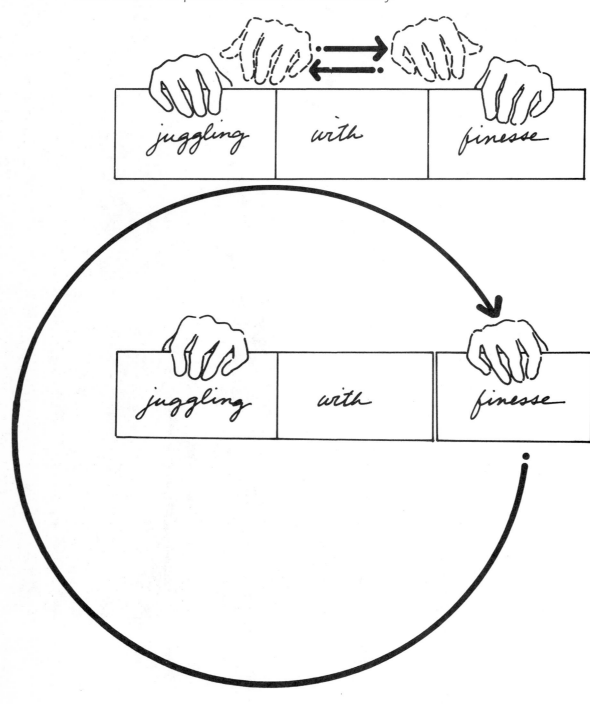

MARK NIZER

SWING BOTH ENDS   Use both end boxes and swing these boxes around the center box so that they do a complete circle and you end up back where you began. You do not have to move fast for this trick. Concentrate especially on the center box.

JUMP OVER ALL 3 BOXES   With the boxes held in front of you, bring them down and jump over all 3 boxes. Then with the boxes behind your back, jump back over them so that they are in front of you once again. To learn this, use a rope and start with it loose so that it hangs low, and jump over the rope. Then keep bringing it tighter as you improve, bring it tighter until it goes straight across from hand to hand. Then try it with the boxes.

JUGGLE 3 BOXES   Juggle 3 boxes in a reverse cascade using half flips. Grab each box with your fingers up and your palms forward. To start the juggle, throw the center box in a single flip straight up, then go into a juggle. Juggle the boxes with your hands high near your face.

3 HELD TOGETHER, SIDEWAYS FLIP   Catch the center box between the other 2 so that they are longer sides against longer side. Once you have them in this position, flip all of them sideways so that the box that will be going to the top as you flip them does a full single flip and the other 2 boxes do half flips. Quickly grab the 2 boxes that do half flips and use these to catch the last box by the suede ends after it does a full flip.

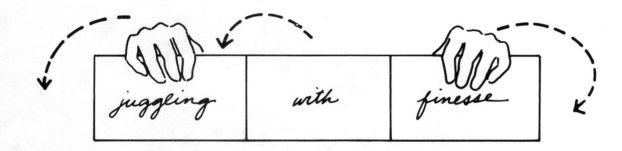

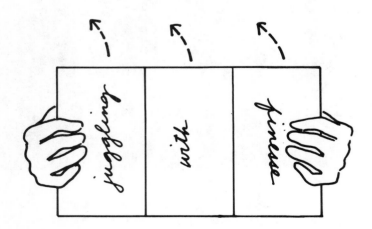

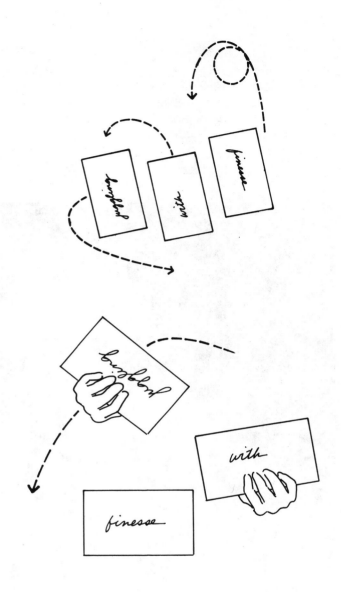

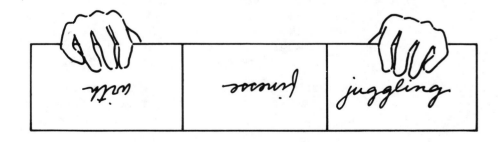

1, 2, 3 UP PIROUETTE   Use 1,2, or 3 boxes to do a pirouette. Get your feet positioned so that you have to pirouette as little as possible. Don't lift the box or boxes very high and you will get more control. Make sure that the boxes stay lined up correctly before you do the pirouette. Do not have a runny nose when you are performing this trick, your audience might get mad at you.

Doing a pirouette with 3 boxes in the air, Kris Kremo.

CIGAR BOX DROPS   There are some good comedy gags with 3 boxes for drops. When a box is dropped, instead of stopping the routine and immediately picking up the box, continue to whack the remaining 2 boxes together, still in time to the music. Then slowly stop and look puzzled at the 2 boxes in your hands, and then look surprised to see the box on the floor. Quickly pick up the missing box and go on with the routine.

DROP # TWO   After dropping a box, put the right and left box against the sides of your head and go through a few moves as though the head were the center box. If you are using a drummer for your act, have him hit a loud beat each time the boxes contact your head.

DROP # THREE   After a box is dropped, juggle the 3 boxes on the stage by picking up the outside box and putting it down in the center of the pattern so that the boxes do a reverse cascade pattern. While doing this, act as if it were part of the act..

GRAB THIRD BOX

Grab the third box away from either end with the opposite hand and place it on the end where your hand started. Then catch the other boxes. Lift the boxes so that the boxes that are going to be in the middle do not separate. You can also do this and catch the whole stack behind your back, or under your leg.

Using 4 boxes, Charley Brown.

PIROUETTE WITH 2 OR 4 BOXES

Lift 2 boxes, or all 4 boxes in the air and turn a pirouette. You have to make sure that the boxes keep from separating when you release them. First practice just throwing 2 boxes, or all 4 boxes so that the boxes do not separate. When doing a pirouette using 4 boxes, make sure to release the boxes completely before turning the pirouette.

TURN END BOXES

As you lift the boxes, turn one of the end boxes a half flip and catch the whole stack again. As you lift the boxes push the whole stack together toward the side that is not turning. Both sides can be turned at the same time also in this manner.

Have the 9 boxes stacked in a straight pile standing in front of you on the floor or on a table. Grab them off with one hand then transfer them to the other hand. Keep the stack going parallel with the ground. You have to be very fast when grabbing the boxes from the straight stack and placing them on the other stack before the boxes fall.

Once you have all the boxes between your hand, set them down on the table, or floor, on their side in a straight line with the long sides up in front of you. Push the center box forward about three inches.

Place one hand on each of the end boxes, near their centers, and get a firm grip on the stack. This is done by pressing them all together very tightly. Lift the boxes up about head high and by controlling the boxes with pressure, mesh them together one side at a time, trading off each side. The ends of the boxes will go against the middle of the box right before it in a hinge-like motion. When all of the boxes are meshed together, place 2 boxes under the pile of boxes and balance the whole stack on your chin (you might want to reread the chapter on balancing). After balancing the boxes, bring them down with your hands and hold the 2 boxes that were on the bottom of the balance flat against the rest of the stack. Then tilt each hand away from the center so that the boxes separate into two piles, one in each hand.

Once you have two stacks, let them fall together in the center, catch them in one straight stack between your hands. Finally, throw the stack up and do a pirouette before catching the stack of boxes again.

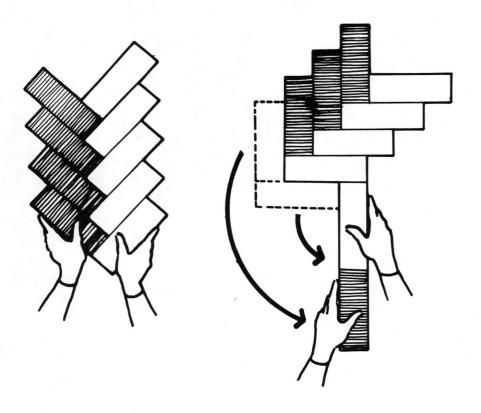

• MORE PROPS •

Here is an additional listing of props that can be juggled, just to give you ideas.

basketballs	hatchets	tennis rackets	marbles
volleyballs	butcher knives	badminton rackets	plates
footballs	baseball bats	playing cards	bowling balls
daggers	water	straight sticks	frogs

Ray Jason, 4 basketballs.

Michael Chirrick

Michael Chirrick, juggling 4 volleyballs and bouncing 1 on his forehead.

Kit Summers, using 4 rackets.

3 plates, Tommy Curtin.

5 plates in the air, George Lerch.

Ron Meyers, not struggling with 3 bowling balls.

NINE
JUGGLING ON DIFFERENT VEHICLES

You do not have to juggle while always standing on the ground. There are various props and vehicles that can be used as a base to juggle, adding interest and excitement to the show. I have seen, heard of, or actually done myself, juggling on these vehicles listed. But I am just touching on a few ideas that you can work on.

Unicycle   To learn to ride a unicycle, get on and support yourself by holding onto a wall or something solid. You have to keep your back straight and look straight forward. To control the unicycle you use your hips against each side of the seat. At first ride next to a wall and use it for support when needed. Then work on riding in the open. Remember to keep looking forward and to keep your back straight. To learn to juggle while you are riding the unicycle you have to learn to isolate your arms so that they can be used for the juggling. First, practice riding with your hands crossed in front of you. You must use your hips and thighs quite a bit when you ride and juggle. It is important to be relaxed as much as possible when riding a unicycle. One trick I included in my act was jumping rope while on the unicycle. I used toe straps on the peddles to hold my feet. If you want to learn all about the unicycle, building them, learning tricks, and history, a very good book on the subject is **THE UNICYCLE BOOK,** written by my friend, Jack Wiley.

Daniel Rosen riding a unicycle, on the ice!

High Unicycle   Learning to ride a tall unicycle (A unicycle that has the peddles extended above the wheel) is mostly just a matter of getting over your fear of the height. With the height advantage you have more time to control a fall; therefore it is easier to juggle on a high unicycle. When you first start learning to ride a high unicycle, just ride forward about five feet and then fall off. This will help you get over your fear of falling from the unicycle. Once again you have to remember to use your hips and thighs against the seat to control the unicycle.

Rudy Horn did a great routine on a tall unicycle. As he rocked on one foot, he would use his other foot to kick cups and saucers up to land on his head.

I performed using a seven-foot unicycle when I was doing street shows. I learned when I was thirteen and became proficient at an early age. Jon Held and I used to pass 6 clubs while rocking on high unicycles. I built a fourteen foot unicycle while I was in high school. I used it for a few shows and for just riding around, but it was not practical and I finally sold it. I hope that the guy that bought it from me is still all right!

3 torches on a high unicycle during a street show, Kit Summers.

Slack Rope or Tight Wire

The kind of shoes that you use for walking on the rope is very important. The shoes should conform to your feet and the rope. A thin leather shoe is the best. Slack rope walking requires a limber body because you always have to be moving on the rope. So it helps to do a good stretch-out before you walk. When first learning to juggle on the rope, have the rope just a few inches off the ground. Use a mat underneath the rope in case you fall. Keep your knees bent while on the rope. Keep your weight low while walking. Learn to balance on each foot individually first. When walking on the rope you have to have a slow transfer of weight from foot to foot. You have to learn to isolate the top and bottom half of your body, so that the top half does the juggling, and the bottom half controls you on the rope. Most of the time while you are juggling on the rope, you will be standing on one leg, using the other leg for balance. Make your throws very accurate because as you know, the body cannot move very much to make a save.

These days, one of the best on the slack rope is Dan Wiles from San Diego. He can juggle 5 clubs while spinning two rings on the rope, do a half pirouette with 4 clubs, and do a very good 3 club routine. I have coached Dan a great deal on his act, and I have seen a wonderful improvement.

Varga Pavlova, on the slack rope.

Cliff Spengor, slack rope juggling.

Horse   You will have to use your legs quite a bit when juggling while standing on a moving horse. Keep your knees bent, to compensate for the up and down motion of the horse. Try to keep the horse at a smooth walk. Wind is a factor when you juggle on a moving horse, so be ready for it. Also, you could tie the horse up and put his feet in cement to keep him from moving around. To juggle on a kid's toy rocking horse you have to learn to juggle while moving in a forward and backward motion.

Juggling on horseback, the Dunais.

Tap Dance   First purchase some tap dance shoes. Next take dance lessons. It looks, and sounds very good to do a tap dance routine while juggling. Your hands will make a tapping sound also if you wear rings while you are juggling clubs. For a time, Bobby May included this in his act.

Hang by Hair and Juggle   Braid your hair together and then use a hook to connect the braid to a cable (Ouch!). Have the cable and yourself lifted into the air and juggle. It also looks good to be swinging while hanging by your hair and juggling.

CHRYS HOLT   RINGLING BROTHERS and BARNUM & BAILEY CIRCUS
MADISON SQUARE GARDEN, NEW YORK

Unsupported Ladder   Use a ladder that is about five or six feet in height. Have one leg in front and one leg behind while standing above it on about the third rung. You will have to keep the ladder rocking back and forth to keep it balanced. It helps to have rings that your feet will fit into to help you keep it rocking.

Gregor Papavitch, 5 clubs on the unsupported ladder.

Rolling Globe   You will always be moving while you are on a rolling globe. Practice until you have complete control over the globe on which you juggle. You have to keep your body straight while juggling on a rolling globe. You will have to be able to juggle and move the globe in any direction.

On the rolling globe, Pemani.

:e Skates or Roller Skates   When skating and juggling you will be moving from side to side as you push and propel yourself forward. The wind is a large factor when doing this, so use heavier props. When juggling on ice it is easiest to get yourself moving and then juggle while you are coasting.

The first time I met Albert Lucas was in 1977 when he was touring with The Ice Capades. He was born in 1960. Albert performed with the Ice Capades for almost ten years, from the age of 12 to age 22. He started juggling at the age of three, taught and coached by his father, Albert Moreira, who was a member (along with Anthony Gatto's father, Nick) of the Los Gattos Trio. It is said that at the age of five Albert was working on juggling 5 balls. Albert Lucas is the only person I have heard of that could juggle the number of objects that is also their age (5). Albert stunned the juggling world by winning all of the competitions he entered at the 1984 International Juggling Convention in Las Vegas. His brother, David Lucas, also performs while on skates. They have both developed marvelous juggling acts on or off the ice.

On ice, Albert Lucas.

Handling 4 rackets on ice, David Lucas.

Daniel Rosen did not want to do the usual stage juggling act. He figured that what he could do to be different was to put his act on ice. He had not skated before that time. He practiced every day, and eventually he was booked with the Ice Capades. Daniel went from the ice on to perform at comedy clubs around the U.S. After a time he was doing mostly comedy and not much juggling. On the ice he performed 5 torches, a nice 3 club routine, and rode a unicycle on the ice using a spiked tire. Daniel and I started juggling at about the same time. If you ever get the chance to meet him you will see what a good juggler and wonderful person he is.

Daniel Rosen, juggling 5 torches on ice.

Bobby May did a very smooth and nice act for a while on ice skates and also roller skates.

At the time I am writing this, Tommy Curtin performs with a group that does a show on portable plastic ice. If you ever get the chance to meet him you will see what a great guy he is.

At one time when I was working on an act on ice, Bobby May wrote me. "About doing an act on ice, I used figure skates. The main idea is to get a good fitting pair of skating shoes and have an expert put the blades on and fit the skates to your feet, as this is very important. I did simple skating maneuvers such as cut backs (which looks very good). You can do around the back gliding backwards and under one leg while skating in a circle going forward. On the ice you must project larger than on a stage as the public is some distance away. Also remember to look up on the finishes and when you are taking bows. In doing juggling-skating, the audience is mainly watching the juggling tricks. I would suggest keeping the skating fairly simple."

Juggling on roller skates, Bobby May.

Stilts   Make stilts that can be strapped onto your legs so that you have your hands free to juggle. You have to keep rocking back and forth to keep yourself balanced. Try an under the leg throw while you are walking on stilts and juggling.

Rola Bola   While juggling on a rola bola, your hands stay in one place, and the lower part of your body does a repetitive arc under your juggling pattern. On tricks in which you throw the object straight up you have to remember that you will be in a different location when the prop comes down once again. With clubs, try an Albert throw or a trebla throw.

Juggling while astride the Rola Bola, Presto the Magic Clown.

TEN
HOW TO PERFORM YOUR ACT

Now that your have practiced your juggling skills and are comfortable with your ability, it's time to pursue the enjoyable art of performance. I have found it to expand my love of juggling.

First, I want to say that you never have to perform your juggling; juggling in itself is very enjoyable, a personal thing. But, once you have shown just one person your juggling, you have performed.

Juggling and performing will give your life a positive attitude. It will open you up to people. Juggling will make you more sure of yourself, and at the same time it can bring in a substantial income. Developing a good act will open a new universe of possibilities and opportunity. With juggling you can travel the world. There really is no limit to where you can go with the act. People the world over enjoy juggling tremendously.

With 3 objects you can amuse and amaze the entire population of the earth, and maybe even the planet Pluto. Don't think that you have to juggle more than 1, 2, or 3 objects to perform an impressive act. Francis Brunn once said, "At one time I did Indian clubs. I also did more hoops than I do now, and worked with smaller balls. I have gone away from this kind of work because I felt very limited. By limited I mean you cannot really use your imagination. The possibilities are fewer. Sure, you can throw hoops, you can do 8 or 9 of them, but the variations are less. So I found with fewer objects there are more possible variations. For myself, I find that I am fascinated by controlling 1 ball. It sounds like nothing, but it is quite difficult to do properly. The body has to be right; the feeling has to be right. There are many things involved. It took me a long time to arrive at this, so it is difficult to explain. It's just a certain feeling I have."

Airjazz — Jon Held, Peter Davison, Kazia Tenembaum. Great on Stage.

Kris Kremo does a superb act in which he juggles either 3 balls, 3 cigar boxes, 1 bowler hat, or 3 hats. After five years of teamwork with his father Bela, he launched out on his own in 1974 and within three years he was already ranked among the best jugglers in the world. His act really radiates charm and a certain brilliance. I met Kris the first time in 1978. Not only is he a great juggler, he is a very warm and friendly person.

Béla Kremo

Kris learned from his father, Bela Kremo.

You can't just juggle in front of people, you really have to perform for them. It is not only the juggling that people are looking at, it is your appearance, personality and the way that you present your act. One of the highlights of the great juggler Massimiliano Truzzi's act was called the pop-corn gag. Truzzi would throw a ball into the audience for someone to throw back, then he would catch the ball (when it was thrown back) on a knife held in his mouth. After doing this a few times he would throw the ball to a man who attempted to catch it and ran into a pop-corn vendor. Pop-corn flew over everyone in the vicinity. He once said, "That's the trouble: people love the pop-corn gag, and it takes no practice. I do six plates and bounce the ball on my forehead after ten years of practice and people say, it's good." That shows you that the presentation portion of your act is equally important.

• PUTTING YOUR ACT TOGETHER AND PRACTICING YOUR ACT •

To work out a good routine for your show, first write down all of the tricks that you know can be done with the prop with which you are working. Even include tricks that you can't do. Then put them in an order that has good transitions from trick to trick, so that your routine flows well. Once you have learned all of the tricks, then throw out (in a cascade, of course) the tricks that you don't like, or tricks that you feel uncomfortable doing. That way you will have learned many tricks, and worked out a good routine for your show. With each routine try to arrange the order so that each routine builds to a climax.

When you are juggling, you really have to have your mind together and be in control. Therefore drinking and drugs do not mix with juggling.

As you are putting your act together, be able to adapt your act to work under a low ceiling, or in any circumstances. You never know where you may be working. You should be able to run your act from five minutes to an hour, so that you have enough material to work in any show. Try to have two hours of material so that you can choose from that for the type of show that you are doing.

When you perform your act it looks impressive to use the whole stage if you can. Use a large variety of movement in your show. Bobby May told me, "Do a trick close to the body, and then a trick that is large and has a lot of movement. Always keep your audience guessing what you are going to do next. If you are playing a big auditorium, exaggerate your gestures and when talking speak up, since in big places everything has to be emphasized more." Gear your show and tricks to the type of showroom that you are working in. If you are working in a circus, make sure that your tricks are large enough for all of the crowd to see. For a smaller crowd you can make your tricks more intricate and detailed. The audience must be able to see and understand what you are doing.

It is a good idea to start your act with something that you are very sure of. That makes the audience sure of your juggling, and gives you confidence. Your whole show will run better if you can show the audience that you are sure of yourself.

If it is possible, audience participation is good to use in your show. Try to get the audience involved somehow. Make them feel that they are part of your show. But be careful who you choose as a volunteer; you never know what your volunteer might do.

Do not perform a trick for too long. The audience might get bored and go home. Do a trick until the audience can see and understand what you are doing, then move on to a different trick. It is better to leave an audience wanting more than bore them with a trick that is done for too long a time. Try to do tricks that the audience can see and understand well. Do not be too repetitious in your juggling.

You can build up any trick. Make it look impossible to the audience, and your act will go over even better. You may even want to miss a trick the first try when performing to build suspense. When putting together a routine, if you have a part in which there is an awkward transition, stop juggling and do another start. This is a good way to get applause at this point in the show.

It is good to have an act that is choreographed to music, and a separate act that is performed with talking. That way you can perform in non-English speaking countries using the music. You should be able to perform anywhere. When looking for music to use in your act, find some music that you enjoy listening to very much. Remember, you are the one that has to hear it most often. It is best to use an instrumental piece, unless you find one in which the words go along with the juggling. You may want to have a good musician arrange it for an orchestra so that it fits your act.

When practicing your act, break it down into routines that you plan to use and practice these. Also practice your whole act together so that you work out good transitions from routine to routine, making your whole act run more smoothly. You have to practice it all together to make sure that you have enough energy to get through the entire act. Practice your act as if you were performing it, using facial expressions and everything. If you do drop in practice, say or do whatever it is you would say or do in the show. Be prepared for when it might happen while performing.

You really have to be practiced in your transitions in order that there is no bungling to mar your show. When concluding a routine, you have to remove your props quickly and gracefully. You should be very smooth when going from one prop to another.

Practice your act in front of a mirror some of the time. Work on facial and body positioning. With a mirror you can also work on timing for the act. It will teach you to be able to look at the audience while you are juggling, rather than just the juggling pattern. If you have access to a video tape recorder, tape your act and see where you need improvement. You can also judge your facial expressions using the machine. Tape some of your shows to see how the show is going. It is hard to critique yourself without seeing it from the audience's point of view.

Doing a show is not just a matter of showing your skill. You also have to have good showmanship. For your show you have to practice your act until you are very sure of the act, and yourself. You must perform for your audience, not just show them your juggling.

When you get booked on stage, the stage crew will be talking in a language that you may not be familiar with. here are a few phrases that they may be using:

Upstage: This refers to the part of the stage that is most distant from the audience.

Downstage: The part of the stage that is nearest the audience.

Stage right: This is the part of the stage that is on your right when you are facing the audience.

Stage left: The left side of the stage when you are facing the audience from the stage.

For stage lighting, remember that the brighter you have it, the better the audience will be able to see you. Try to endure. You do not have to look directly into the lights when you are juggling. Look slightly to the side of where the light is. It is better to have the lighting from the footlights for juggling.

Street shows are a good way to start performing your act. It will give you confidence in your act and yourself. Doing street shows will help develop your act because you have to first gather a crowd, then hold them there for the whole show, and finally get all their money from them. A very good street performer is Robert Nelson, alias, The Butterfly Man. He started street performing in San Francisco, known for its street performing. Robert went on to work the college circuit for a few years. He liked street performing so much he eventually went back to only working the streets. Robert has a character that is a bit crass and insulting on stage. Off stage, he is one of the kindest, friendliest people I know. Another person that does a great street act is Edward Jackman. I have seen Edward develop over the years from an act that was alright, to an act that is superb. Edward went on to do the college circuit with a great act. His juggling is great, and his comedy is wonderful. Helping him with the business of the tour is his beautiful wife, Karen. She helped me out a lot after I had the accident.

THE ROLE OF COMEDY IN YOUR ACT

Bobby May once wrote me, "I believe there is alot of funny stuff which can be done with 3 clubs. The public likes comedy and it is commercial. I am of the opinion that it will open a lot of doors for work."

WE JUGGLE   'TIL WE DROP
THE FLYING KARAMAZOV BROTHERS

To work on comedy and to get good comedy ideas, pick a prop or subject and try to work it in all kinds of different ways so that you end up with something that's funny. You will be able to tell what is good by audience reaction. Don't just make an attempt at humor. If you get a good reaction keep it in, if not then find something else. Remember, language is designed to serve you.

Some suggestions on different topics to start with for comedy are impresssions, story telling, audience participation, and naming the moves that you are doing. Do not make your comedy too complicated for your audience to understand. It is important to find a character to play in your show. Make situations credible. Do things you feel are right for your character. Be different, find your own way. Don't ever worry that someone will "steal" your routine or show, they really can't. Everyone has his or her own style and certain moves or expressions that are his or her's alone and cannot be copied. But always try to put original material together for your show. The following is a listing of examples that you can build on for your show. These are just examples to build on, do not use them word for word; just use the idea. These lines have all been used by street performers for years. When you are saying lines for the show, don't sound as if you are reading from a script. Treat members of the audience like they are your good friends. It makes it easier if you act as if you are talking to just one person. You have to sound like you really mean what you are saying.

Drops

This is a real floor show.

The shade got in my eyes.

A string broke.

I almost dropped that one.

Obviously a defective prop.

Five and a half years of practice shot down the drain.

This act is really picking up, don't you think.

Sorry, shaved tonight and cut my juggler vein.

Dead Audience

It's nothing really. I can tell by the applause.

Oh, thank you, both of you.

This is a traditional applause point.

You can applaud at any time.

If it was on T.V. you'd laugh.

I've never seen dead people stand up before.

Danger

This is not television. You can't change the channel if something goes wrong.

Juggling is a dangerous sport, especially for the spectator.

This is dangerous, and you kids in the audience should never try it...unless, of course, your parents aren't home.

Don't be afraid...I've done this trick...twice.

And now I'm going to risk my life, along with the entire front row.

Heckler Lines

Don't worry folks, every village has one.

Let's play horse. I'll be the front end, and you can be yourself.

Well, there's something that penicillin won't cure.

That's all right, I remember when I had my first beer too.

I have two words to say to you, and they're not "happy birthday."

Miscellaneous Lines

At no point do my hands ever leave my wrists.

Believe me, it's as tough as it looks.

Look at that one! You should see it from back here.

You think you're impressed!

Juggling in this wind is a breeze.

Don't worry, I've done this trick a thousand times...but it's only worked twice.

There are two great jugglers in the country, but that's okay, there's plenty of room for both of us.

Money Lines

I'm not a parking meter, I do accept bills.

My skills are good; my humor is clean; I'm allergic to copper, so give me some green.

Did you want change for those pennies?

Remember, no donation is too small, just fold it up and drop it in.

This is the way I make a living. That's all right though, because the average donation is five dollars.

Please help me send my parents to college.

Think of it just like church, and you Mormons give ten percent.

Do not perform a trick for too long. The audience might get bored and go home. Do a trick until the audience can see and understand what you are doing, then move on to a different trick. It is better to leave an audience wanting more than bore them with a trick that is done for too long a time. Try to do tricks that the audience can see and understand well. Do not be too repetitious in your juggling.

You can build up any trick. Make it look impossible to the audience, and your act will go over even better. You may even want to miss a trick the first try when performing to build suspense. When putting together a routine, if you have a part in which there is an awkward transition, stop juggling and do another start. This is a good way to get applause at this point in the show.

It is good to have an act that is choreographed to music, and a separate act that is performed with talking. That way you can perform in non-English speaking countries using the music. You should be able to perform anywhere. When looking for music to use in your act, find some music that you enjoy listening to very much. Remember, you are the one that has to hear it most often. It is best to use an instrumental piece, unless you find one in which the words go along with the juggling. You may want to have a good musician arrange it for an orchestra so that it fits your act.

Do not be afraid to have fun on stage. If you appear to be enjoying yourself (and I hope you are) the audience will join you and have fun also. Don't just perform with a straight face, not acknowledging the audience. You should try to develop a character on stage. I can't really help you with this; all characters are different.

TOLY M,

If something happens that shouldn't, and you know the audience caught it (let's face it, it happens to the best), retrieve the prop in a graceful manner, pass is off as something funny, or at least acknowledge it smoothly. Some of the audience must have caught it anyway. This is better than getting flustered, or just picking up the prop and continuing. If you drop, be ready with a line, or expression for the audience. Have something prepared beforehand so that you are ready. Be relaxed and take your time.

There is no need or reason to be too nervous before, or during a show. Think of it more just as your being out having a good time. Do acknowledge that the audience is there, just keep your mind together and do a good show. Above all, have confidence in yourself and your show. You should be up for the show. Just don't be overly nervous.

You must show a sense of confidence. Be in control of the whole situation. In a way you have to overpower the audience. Show enthusiasm in what you do. When you are on stage, try to be the master of everything that is going on, at the same time you must be enjoying yourself. As you are juggling you have to not only see the props, but you have to see the whole show, or you lose sight of the props. Have an overall view of everything that is going on.

You can feel either that the audience is on your side, or that they are against you. You always have to remember that they are on your side. It is not you against the audience. You may have a bad audience for one show, but always remember that you will be doing shows in the future.

At all costs avoid injuring your spectators in any way, either physically or mentally. Be in control of your juggling and what you're saying at all times.

You have to dress nice and keep clean on stage, as well as off stage, so that you always make a good impression. Keep your props clean and in good condition. When you are putting together a costume, make sure that you can move well in it for your entire act. You have to be very comfortable in your costume. It is good to use a costume for your act because a costume impresses people. You can't just look like a person off the street. Your costume you should match the character that you portray in your show. Find one that fits you and your act. Be sure that the costume is easily cleanable.

When you start performing on stage, it is a good idea to use stage makeup. You really do need it for stage. First use a pancake base to cover your whole face. Then apply a little rouge to your upper cheeks. After this use an eyebow pencil to apply coloring to your eyebrows. Last of all, use a tissue to wipe off your lips. Now you are ready to face the audience.

Juggling is similar to dancing. Move with the juggling. Remember people are not just watching the juggling, they are watching you. The juggling should come second to your performing. And please learn to smile; facial expression is so important.

As you perform use a prop stand. This looks classier than having your props lying on the stage. To design your prop stand, figure out exactly what props you would like to use in your act. Then use this information to design your prop stand, allowing room for every prop. You must design it so that it can be transported easily. You can also use a large bag or container that can stand on its own for discarding used props. If you can't complete a trick in three tries, go on to the next trick. You don't want the audience to suffer through your misses. You should try to flow and be smooth in your show.

When the audience is really enjoying themselves as they are watching you, do a finish and take a bow, then start up juggling again. Take this time to acknowledge their applause. They will see that you know you are doing well and feel that they are a part of your success.

While you are bowing for an audience, put your heart and soul into your bow. Let the people know that you love them. Really show the people that you appreciate them enjoying you and your juggling. When the audience is applauding for you, don't join them and applaud along with them; it looks too much like you are applauding yourself. Just gratefully accept their caring and applause.

Do each performance as if it were going to be your last. Put everything that you can into the show. If you bomb in your first shows, don't be too upset. It takes time to develop a good act. Just sit down and figure out why you bombed, then correct it before the next show. All audiences are different. You may have just had a bad crowd. There are live audiences and dead ones. You should be able to determine which you have when you first go on. Once you have this information, gear your show to the type of audience you have.

• BOOKING YOUR ACT AND ON THE ROAD •

Now that you have your act together (as they say), you have to book the act. This is not so difficult as you might think. People all over the world love juggling acts. Juggling has taken me across the country four times, to Europe, and to Hawaii. There are job opportunities everywhere. You just have to do a little searching for them.

First, get 8 by 10 photos taken of yourself. Have a close body shot from the waist up and a full body action shot taken while juggling. Have your name printed at the bottom of the picture. Stamp your address and phone number on the back so that people will be able to contact you when they have work for you.

TWO THROWING TABORS

=PERMANENT ADDRESS=

135 FOOTS AVE.

JAMESTOWN, NEW YORK.

Get a resume printed up. Don't use a copy. You have to present yourself in a high class manner. List the best of your past performances, starting with the most recent. Tell something about the act that you are presently doing. Be sure to include your name and address on it. The following example is a resume that I once used:

KIT SUMMERS

"Juggling with Finesse"

4464 Castelar St., Apt. 320   Phone: (619) 224-3887
San Diego, CA 92107

VARIOUS EXPERIENCE, AND PERFORMANCES

Television: "The Gong Show" NBC television (first place); Hollywood, CA
                  Channels 8, 10, and 39 television news; San Diego, CA
                  Commercial for Ala Moana Shopping Center; Honolulu, HI

Stage: San Diego Civic Light Opera, "Carousel"; San Diego, CA
                  University of California at San Diego; San Diego, CA
                  Paradise Park; Honolulu, HI
                  Tour Ship Queen Mary; Long Beach, CA
                  Sheffield Music Hall; London, England
                  Vineyard Shopping Center; Escondido, CA
                  Ala Moana Shopping Center; Honolulu, HI
                  University Town Center Shopping Center; San Diego, CA
                  Seaport Village; San Diego, CA
                  Victorian Fun Fair; Descanso, CA
                  Ballys Park Place Hotel and Casino; Atlantic City, NJ

Teaching: Juggling instructor for Ringling Brothers and Barnum and Bailey
                  Clown College; Venice, FL
                  Juggling class at Honolulu recreation center; Honolulu, HI
                  Grape Festival; Escondido, CA

Peter Marshall
said: "I was stunned, it was really good to see his act."

Eva Gabor: "He is absolutely marvelous, incredible."

Arte Johnson: "I think that young people that do this kind of work are
                  extraordinary, Kit is just marvelous."

Current juggling
act: The act is a fast paced juggling act combining comedy, dance,
                  and juggling with balls, clubs, rings, tennis rackets,
                  machetes, and flaming torches; unicycling.

Special
strengths: Juggling, unicycling, balancing, improvisation, acting,
                  modeling.

Physical
statistics: Height; 6 feet
                  Weight; 165 pounds
                  Hair; Blonde
                  Eyes; Blue
                  Complexion; Light

A sample resume the author used for a number of years.

Make a video tape of your act to send out if necessary. Try to tape a live show if possible. The video may be as short as five minutes. You only have to show what you are capable of doing. Tape a couple of shows so that you can edit your best together. Give your photo and resume to schools, shopping centers, colleges, and all the talent agents in the area. Each contact will introduce you to others that might be able to book you.

If you need to save money, use the college system in our city. Many times the students need projects to work on. Think of it as a charitable act. Go to the photography department and ask if there is a student to work with. That way you give someone a project, and you get free photography. Also go to the media/ department and talk to the teacher. If a student needs a video project, set up a show at the school with a couple of classes watching. They get a free show, and you get a live audience.

Whenever you do a show for a place of business, always ask for a letter of recommendation to include with your photo and resume. When a newspaper does a story on you and includes a photo, ask for the negatives, or copies of all the shots. They may have some good shots that they did not include with the article. When a television station does a story on you, ask for a copy of your segment of the program. They will probably be happy to oblige you.

If your performing calls for a lot of traveling, use a car or a camper that will hold all of your things easily. You also should be able to pack and unpack quickly and easily. It is important to be very comfortable traveling in the vehicle.

When you have a new booking, test out the stage and the lighting before you do your act. Stages are different everywhere. Don't just go out and perform without knowing all the conditions.

If it is possible, it is best to set your own props, to make sure they are all accounted for and properly in place. Remember, you are the one who has to pick them up and use them.

As you are doing a stage show, if you are talking, the stage crew will usually supply a stand-up microphone. Find out if they can get a cordless, clip-on mike for you to use. A cordless clip-on mike is the best to use for juggling. You might want to purchase one yourself to use in stage shows. But then again, you might have a good comedy routine using the stand-up mike as a prop.

So now that your act is all together, get some bookings and hit the road. But, above all, have fun with it.

• SUMMARY: PERFORMING YOUR ACT •

— Develop a good act that can run from five to thirty minutes.

— Get a pleasing costume made that fits your act and your character.

— Make sure that your props and stage setting look nice.

— Get photos, resume, and a video made of your act.

— Send out publicity to all agents, schools, shopping centers and everywhere else you can think of in the area.

— Have a great time.

PROP MAKERS AND THE I.J.A.

The advancement in making props over the last decade has helped advance juggling. Manufacturers of equipment are still making advances in the development of juggling props all of the time. If you are seriously interested in becoming a juggler, I recommend that you buy quality equipment. It will help you to improve faster. Inferior props only hinder your progress and will eventually have to be replaced. Modern technology now allows the production of highly uniform and carefully balanced equipment, unavailable to jugglers in the past. Thus, new juggling records are being set everyday.

Here is a list of prop makers who will sell you equipment. Write and ask them to send you a catalog. Each prop maker carries most of the props in this book.

Brian Dube
25 Park Place
New York City, New York 10007
(212) 619-2182

Stuart Raynolds
2415 Ramblewood Drive
Wilmington, Delaware 19810
(302) 475-6643

Todd Smith
13401 Lake Shore Blvd.
Cleveland, Ohio 44120
(216) 283-1815

Ben Decker
4025 John Street
San Diego, California 92106
(619) 222-0100

Juggle Bug
7506 J Olympic View Drive
Edmonds, Washington 98020
(206) 774-2127

The International Jugglers Association is an organization that began in 1947. It is the major organization for juggling in the world, and offers a juggling magazine, JUGGLER'S WORLD, that is published quarterly. It contains useful information about juggling. The association has a convention annually in various cities around the United States, and the number of members is increasing each year. The address of the International Jugglers Association is:

International Jugglers Association
P.O. Box 29
Kenmore, New York 14217

"The big toss up" at an IJA convention.

Many different terms have been used over the years for the various juggling tricks. This chapter interprets some of the most common.

Cascade — The throws are thrown underneath and to the inside of the preceding throw. This is the basic juggling pattern. It is the first step when learning to juggle and serves as a base for the juggling pattern.

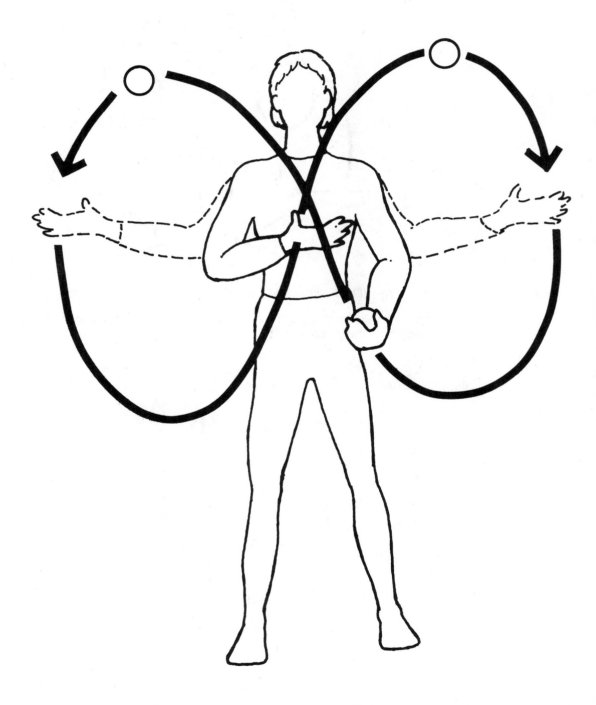

Columns — The throws are thrown in a straight line up and down.

Flash — There are two definitions for this word. It is either just doing the number of throws of the amount of props that you are using. Or quickly throw all of the props that you are using into the air so that they are airborn at the same time.

Flat throw — (Done with clubs or rings, not done with balls). Throws are tossed with the prop held, and thrown, parallel with the shoulders, rather than at right angles to the body.

Floater — (Done with clubs.) The club is thrown so that it does not spin at all.

Fountain — The throws are thrown and caught with the same hand, so that they do not cross the center point.

Half Shower — One side throws underneath and to the inside. The other hand throws over the top and to the outside.

Lift — You bring the prop that you are using straight up using your entire arm more than your wrist.

Multiplex — The throwing and catching of more than one object at a time with either hand.

Off-sync — Throws are thrown with each hand throwing at different times.

Sync — Synchronized, both hands throw at the same time.

On-Sync — Same as Sync.

Pirouette — To turn a complete circle with the body.

Reverse cascade — The throws go over the top and to the outside of the preceding throw with each hand.

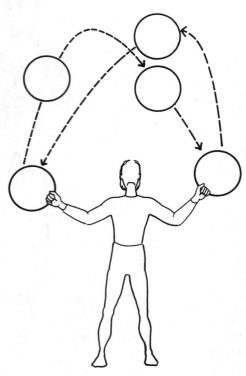

Shower — One hand makes all the throws while the second catches and quickly passes back to the first, so that they do a circle.

Solids — Every throw from each hand is the designated trick.

Spread — Basically the same as columns; the throws are thrown on sync so that one pair of columns is next to the other.

KATIA ALCARESE   * La Juggler Classique *

Trip — (Done with clubs). Triple, or three spins.

Quad — (Done with clubs). Quadruple, or four spins.

Mill — (Done with clubs). Million, or 1,000,000 spins.

• ALPHABETICAL INDEX OF PUBLICITY PHOTOGRAPHS •

Living with Finesse: Strategies for Success

Speaking of speaking, Kit Summers is not only writing books these days, he is also a speaker for corporations, associations, professional groups, and schools. Kit has been in the entertainment field for over 15 years. He incorporates juggling and magic to use as a medium for presenting a variety of messages to enhance effectiveness, increase productivity, and achieve maximum results in others. His inspirational approach is highly motivating, as well as entertaining.

Kit emphasizes three major themes in his program:

A. Breaking through self-imposed barriers and attaining greater self-confidence.
B. Goal setting to achieve your wants and desires in life—business and personal.
C. Viewing changes in life as opportunities rather than barriers, to grow and learn from.

An attentive audience is a stimulated audience. Kit stimulates his audience to discuss, to remember, to apply, and to benefit from refreshing, useful ideas. The benefits are limitless as you learn how to wake up your mind to eliminate self-imposed restrictions. Dynamic and innovative, he leaves participants thinking, laughing and anxious to apply what they've learned to being more productive, effective and creative in their business, as well as personal life. Using humor, he gently reminds us that growth depends on our ability to learn from past experiences and move forward with finesse to the promise of a good future.

Kit shows people that any obstacle may be overcome, if they will only persevere with the attainable goals they set for themselves. This is from personal experience: Kit progressed from total paralysis back to his former abilities as a juggler by the systematic setting and achieving of goals.

Life is full of changes: business transactions, communication, technological changes, relationships, accidents, et cetera. In this presentation you will learn ideas on how to positively adjust to changes in life; you will gain insight on how to tap your inner resources to see change as an avenue of constructive growth. Kit is a dynamic speaker who believes learning to overcome can be fun!

His format may be custom-designed to meet the needs of your function. Kit Summers designs a high-quality, high-impact presentation that is tailored to your group. He motivates, instructs and entertains throughout the country with his powerful presentation. Now Kit Summers is available to speak to your group.

Kit Summers
2068 Via Las Cumbres, Suite 7
P.O. Box 11244
San Diego, CA 92111
(619) 569-7728

— ADDITIONAL COPIES —

If not available at your local bookstore, you may order additional copies of **"JUGGLING WITH FINESSE"** BY Kit Summers directly from the publisher. If you wish, we will ship to another person with a GIFT CARD from you.

SEND TO:
FINESSE PRESS
2068 Via Las Cumbres #7
P.O. Box 11244
San Diego, CA 92111

Please ship _____ copie(s) of "Juggling With Finesse" at $14.95, plus $1.50 shipping for each book = $_____.

California residents add 6% tax. If you wish fast, first class shipping, add $2.50 per book.

☐ CASH   ☐ VISA   NO. _____

☐ CHECK   ☐ MASTERCARD   EXPIRATION _____

☐ MONEY ORDER   SIGNATURE _____

NAME _____

ADDRESS _____

CITY _____ STATE _____ ZIP _____

☐ PLEASE INCLUDE GIFT CARD   ☐ DO NOT ENCLOSE GIFT CARD

SEND TO _____

ADDRESS _____

CITY _____ STATE _____ ZIP _____

SEND TO _____

ADDRESS _____

CITY _____ STATE _____ ZIP _____

SEND TO _____

ADDRESS _____

CITY _____ STATE _____ ZIP _____

— IF NECESSARY, ATTACH A SEPARATE SHEET OF PAPER —